Sack and Des

ot the

City of Columbia, S. C.

By Wm. Gilmore Simms

To Which is Added

A List of the Property Destroyed.

The Confederate Reprint Company

www.confederatereprint.com

Columbia, S. C.:
Power Press of Daily Phoenix,
1865.

Reprinted 2000

Printed in Dixie.
Deo Vindice!

For a catalogue listing of other available titles,
or for wholesale discounts, please contact:

The Confederate Reprint Company

Post Office Box 386 Dahlonega, Georgia 30533

e-mail: sales@confederatereprint.com
website: www.confederatereprint.com

HOME, SWEET HOME.

A correspondent of the Augusta *Constitutionalist* states that a young lady, whose house was destroyed and burned by Sherman's army while at Columbia, a day or two after the conflagration, visited the ruins, in hopes of finding some little relic to remind her of the trials through which she had passed. She searched in vain, until her eye fell on a small piece of paper, which she picked up. It proved to be a remnant of John Howard Payne's song of "Home, Sweet Home," and the only words that were left untouched by the flames, were:

"THERE IS NO PLACE LIKE HOME."

Not one little relic—not a souvenir left!
Of all that she lov'd by the mad flames bereft!
The ruins, all blacken'd, loom up on the sky,
And the South wind sings softly their sad lullaby.

She looks here, she looks there, for one little thing;
A letter, a trinket, a ribband or ring;
Perchance there may be 'mid the rubbish and dust,
The miniature features of him she loved first.

No, nothing! the flames, in their savage career,
Have swallow'd up all that her heart holds most dear;
Of her once happy home not a vestige is seen;
The still wind now moans through the crimpt evergreen.

A slip of white paper lay trembling alone
Amid the charr'd timber and smoke-blacken'd stone;
Like a snow-flake on Hecla, it shone in the light,
Or a pearl that was set in the dark brow of night.

The lady took up the lone slip from the ground,
And gazing upon its white surface she found
These six little words, (as if traced by some gnome
To mock her deep grief,) *"There is no place like home."*

Aye, sing of sweet home, 'mid its ashes and smoke,
'Twas bless'd till the spoiler its wailings awoke;
'Twas happy till Northmen, with wild fiendish hate,
Gave towns to the flames and made fields desolate.

J. H. H.

CHAPTER I.

INTRODUCTION.

It has pleased God, in that Providence which is so inscrutable to man, to visit our beautiful city with the most cruel fate which can ever befall States or cities. He has permitted an invading army to penetrate our country almost without impediment; to rob and ravage our dwellings, and to commit three-fifths of our city to the flames. Eighty-four squares out of one hundred and twenty-four (?) which the city contains, have been destroyed, with scarcely the exception of a single house. The ancient capitol building of the State[1]—that venerable structure, which, for seventy years, has echoed with the eloquence and wisdom of the most famous statesmen—is laid in ashes; six temples of the Most High God have shared the same fate; eleven banking establishments; the schools of learning, the shops of art and trade, of invention and manufacture; shrines equally of religion, benevolence and industry; are all buried together, in one congregated ruin. Humiliation spreads her ashes over our homes and garments, and the universal wreck exhibits only one common aspect of despair. It is for us, as succinctly but as fully as possible, and in the simplest language, to endeavor to make the melancholy record of our wretchedness as complete as possible.[2]

---

[1] The old State House was constructed between 1786 and 1790. James Hoban, a young Irishman, who had emigrated to Charleston shortly after the Revolution, was the architect. Upon the recommendation of Henry Laurens, President Washington engaged him to design the executive mansion in Washington. Old pictures of the two buildings show architectural similarities.

[2] Major George Ward Nichols, aid-de-camp to General Sherman, in *The Story of the Great March*, gloats over the wanton destruction by his associates in the following words:

"Columbia will have bitter cause to remember the visit of Sherman's army. Even if peace and prosperity soon return to the land, not in this generation nor the next—no, not for a century—can this city or the state recover from the deadly blow which has taken its life. It is not alone in the property that has been destroyed—the buildings, bridges, mills, railroads, material of every description—nor in the loss of the slaves, who, within the last few days, have joined us by hundreds and thousands—al-

CHAPTER II.

FATAL BLUNDER—REMOVAL OF GENERAL JOHNSTON FROM THE COMMAND OF THE CONFEDERATE ARMY.

When, by a crime, no less than blunder, General Johnston was removed from the command of the Confederate armies in Georgia, which he had conducted with such signal ability, there were not a few of our citizens who felt the impending danger, and trembled at the disastrous consequences which they partly foresaw. The removal of a General so fully in the confidence of his troops, who had so long baffled the conquests, if he could not arrest the march, of the opposing army, was of itself a proceeding to startle the thoughtful mind. General Sherman declared his satisfaction at the event, and on repeated occasions since has expressed himself to the same effect. He was emboldened by the change, and almost instantly after, his successes became rapid and of the most decided character.

General Johnston was by nature, no less than training and education, the very best of the Confederate generals to be opposed to General Sherman. To the nervo-sanguine temperament, eager and impetuous, of the latter, he opposed a moral and physical nature—calm, sedate, circumspect; cool, vigilant and wary—always patient and watchful of his moment—never rash or precipitate, but ever firm and decisive—his resources all regu‹ lated by a self-possessed will, and a mind in full possession of that military *coup d'oeil* which, grasping the remotest relations

---

though this deprivation of the means by which they lived is of incalculable importance—that the most blasting, withering blow has fallen.. It is in the crushing downfall of their inordinate vanity, their arrogant pride, that the rebels will feel the effects of the visit of our army. Their fancied unapproachable, invincible security has been ruthlessly overthrown. Their boasting, threatenings, and denunciations have passed by us like the idle wind. The feet of one hundred thousand abolitionists, hated and despised, have pressed heavily upon their sacred soil, and their spirit is broken. I know that thousands of South Carolina's sons are in the army of the rebellion; but she has already lost her best blood there. Those who remain have no homes. The Hamptons, Barnwells, Simses, Rhetts, Singletons, Prestons, have no homes. The ancient homesteads where were gathered sacred associations, the heritages of many generations, are swept away. When first these men became traitors they lost honor; today they have no local habitations; in the glorious future of this country they will have no name."

In this display of inferiority complex Nichols not only demonstrated his lack of prophetic vision, but lost his sneer at Simms by spelling his name incorrectly. He also sustains Simms and Hampton as against Sherman and Hitchcock.

of the field, is, probably, the very first essential to a general having the control of a large and various army.

The error which took Hood into the colder regions of Tennessee, at the beginning of the winter, was one which the Yankee general was slow to imitate, especially as, in so moving, Hood necessarily left all the doors wide open which conducted to the seaboard. It required no great effort of genius to prompt the former to take the pathways which were thus laid open to him. Even had he not already conceived the propriety of forcing his way to the Atlantic coast, and to a junction with his shipping, the policy of then doing so would have been forced upon him by the proceeding of his rival, and by the patent fact that there were no impediments to such a progress. We had neither army nor general ready to impede his march. It suggested itself. The facility of such a progress was clear enough, and, with that quickness of decision which distinguishes the temperament of Sherman, he at once rushed into the open pathway.

The hasty levies of regular troops, collected by Hardee, and the clans of scattered militia, gathered with great difficulty and untrained to service, were rather calculated to provoke his enterprise than to impede his march, and, laying waste as he went, after a series of small and unimportant skirmishes, he made his way to the coast, made himself master of Savannah, and from the banks of that river, beheld, opened before him, all the avenues into and through South Carolina. It is understood that Hardee had in hand, to oppose this progress, something less than ten thousand men, while the force of Sherman was, in round numbers, something like fifty thousand, of which thirty-three thousand consisted of infantry—the rest of artillery and cavalry.

CHAPTER III.

TERRIBLE FOREBODINGS—SHERMAN'S MARCH THROUGH GEORGIA.

The destruction of Atlanta, the pillaging and burning of other towns of Georgia, and the subsequent devastation along the march of the Federal army through Georgia, gave sufficient earnest of the treatment to be anticipated by South Carolina, should the same commander be permitted to make a like progress in our State. The Northern press furnished him the *cri de guerre* to be sounded when he should cross our borders. "*Voe victis!*"—wo to the conquered!—in the case of a people who had first raised the banner of secession. "The howl of delight," (such was the language of the Northern press,) sent up by Sherman's legions, when they looked across the Savannah to the shores of Carolina, was the sure forerunner of the terrible fate which threatened our people should the soldiers be once let loose upon our lands. Our people felt all the danger. They felt that it required the first abilities, the most strenuous exertions, the most prompt and efficient reinforcements, to prevent the threatening catastrophe.

Hardee, though of acknowledged ability, and considered able as the leader of a corps, was not the man to grasp the business of a large army. All eyes looked to General Johnston as the one man, next to Lee, to whom the duty should be confided and the trust. It was confidently hoped and believed that he would be restored to the command, and that adequate reinforcements would be furnished. At all events, no one doubted that, with adequate supplies of men and material, Johnston would most effectually arrest the farther progress of Sherman's army.

Applications of the most urgent entreaty were addressed by our delegates and leading men in the Confederate Congress to President Davis, urging these objects. But he declined to restore the commander whom he had so greatly wronged, and, in respect to reinforcements, these were too tardily furnished, and in too small number to avail much in offering requisite resistance. The reinforcements did not make their appearance in due season for a concentration of the strength at any one point, and opposition to Sherman, everywhere, consisted of little more than a series of small skirmishes, without result on either side. No pass was held with any tenacity; no battle fought; Sherman was allowed to travel one hundred and fifty miles of our State, through a region of swamp and thicket, in no portion of which could a field be found adequate to the display of ten thousand men, and where, under good partisan leaders, the Federals might have been cut off in separate bodies, their supplies stopped, their march constantly embarrassed by hard fighting, and where, a bloody toll exacted at every defile, they must have found a Thermopylae at every five miles of their march. The Confederates had no partisan fighting, as in days of old. They had a system, which insisted upon artillery as paramount—insisted upon arbitrary lines for defence, chosen without any regard to the topography of the country. "We will make a stand," said the Confederate chiefs, "at this river crossing or that; then fall back to the next river, and so on to the last." Although in a thousand places of dense swamp, narrow defile, and almost impenetrable thicket, between these rivers, it would have been easy to find spots where three hundred men, under competent commanders, who knew the country, might most effectually have baffled three thousand.

CHAPTER IV.

SHERMAN'S ENTRANCE INTO SOUTH CAROLINA—DESTRUCTION OF PROPERTY IN THE LOW-COUNTRY.

The march of the Federals into our State was characterized by such scenes of license, plunder and general conflagration, as very soon showed that the threats of the Northern press, and of their soldiery, were not to be regarded as mere *brutum fulmen*. Day by day brought to the people of Columbia tidings of atrocities committed, and more extended progress. Daily did long trains of fugitives line the roads, with wives and children, and horses and stock and cattle, seeking refuge from the pursuers. Long lines of wagons covered the highways. Half-naked people cowered from the winter under bush tents in the thickets, under the eaves of houses, under the railroad sheds, and in old cars left them along the route. All these repeated the same story of suffering, violence, poverty and nakedness. Habitation after habitation, village after village—one sending up its signal flames to the other, presaging for it the same fate—lighted the winter and midnight sky with crimson horrors.

No language can describe nor can any catalogue furnish an adequate detail of the wide-spread destruction of homes and property. Granaries were emptied, and where the grain was not carried off, it was strewn to waste under the feet of the cavalry or consigned to the fire which consumed the dwelling. The negroes were robbed equally with the whites of food and clothing. The roads were covered with butchered cattle, hogs mules and the costliest furniture. Valuable cabinets, rich pianos, were not only hewn to pieces, but bottles of ink, turpentine, oil, whatever could efface or destroy, was employed to defile and ruin. Horses were ridden into the houses. People were forced from their beds, to permit the search after hidden treasures.

The beautiful homesteads of the parish country, with their wonderful tropical gardens, were ruined; ancient dwellings of black cypress, one hundred years old, which had been reared by the fathers of the republic—men whose names were famous in Revolutionary history—were given to the torch as recklessly as were the rude hovels; choice pictures and works of art, from Europe, select and numerous libraries, objects of peace wholly, were all destroyed. The inhabitants, black no less than white, were left to starve, compelled to feed only upon the garbage to be found in the abandoned camps of the soldiers. The corn scraped up from the spots where the horses fed, has been the only means of life left to thousands but lately in affluence.

And thus plundering, and burning, the troops made their way through a portion of Beaufort into Barnwell District, where they pursued the same game. The villages of Buford's Bridge, of Barnwell, Blackville, Graham's, Bamberg, Midway, were more or less destroyed; the inhabitants everywhere left homeless and without food. The horses and mules, all cattle and hogs, whenever fit for service or for food, were carried off, and the rest shot. Every implement of the workman or the farmer, tools, plows, hoes, gins, looms, wagons, vehicles, was made to feed the flames.

From Barnwell to Orangeburg and Lexington was the next progress, marked everywhere by the same sweeping destruction. Both of these court towns were partially burned.

CHAPTER V.

DOUBTS AND FEARS—FUGITIVES FROM THE LOW-COUNTRY.

These tidings duly reached the people of Columbia, and might have prepared them for the treatment they were destined to receive. Daily accessions of fugitives, bringing with them their

valuables and provisions, made ample report of the progress of
the Federal army. Hundreds of families had seasonably left long
before, in anticipation of the danger. Columbia was naturally
held to be one of the most secure places of refuge. It was never
doubted that this capital city, which contained so many of the
manufactures of the Confederate Government, the Treasury,
&c., would be defended with all the concentrated vigor of which
the Confederacy was capable, especially, too, as upon the several
railroads connected with the city, the army of Lee and the safety
of Richmond were absolutely dependent. Young women of family were sent in large numbers to a city, where numbers seemed to promise a degree of security not to be hoped for in any
obscure rural abode. The city was accordingly doubled in population, and here also was to be found an accumulation of wealth,
in plate, jewels, pictures, books, manufactures of art and *virtu,*
not to be estimated—not, perhaps, to be paralleled in any other
town of the Confederacy. In many instances, the accumulations
were those of a hundred years—of successive generations—in
the hands of the oldest families of the South. A large proportion of the wealth of Charleston had been stored in the capital
city, and the owners of these treasures, in many instances, were
unable to effect any farther remove. If apprehensive of the danger, they could only fold their hands, and, hoping against hope,
pray for escape from a peril to which they could oppose no
farther vigilance or effort.

Still, the lurking belief with most persons, who apprehended
the approach of the Federal army, encouraged the faith that,
as the city was wholly defenceless, in the event of a summons,
it would be surrendered upon the usual terms, and that these
would necessarily insure the safety of non-combatants and protect their property.

But, in truth, there was no small portion of the inhabitants
who denied or doubted, almost to the last moment, that Sherman contemplated any serious demonstration upon the city.
They assumed—and this idea was tacitly encouraged, if not believed, by the authorities, military and civil—that the movement on Columbia was but a feint, and that the bulk of his
army was preparing for a descent upon Charleston. This also
seemed to be the opinion in Charleston itself.

CHAPTER VI.

THE FEDERAL ARMY APPROACHING COLUMBIA—SKIRMISHING— CHEATHAM AND STEWART EXPECTED.

All these conjectures were speedily set at rest, when, on the 13th February, (Monday,) the Federal army was reported to have reached a point in Lexington District, some ten miles above Jeffcoat's. On the 14th, their progress brought them to Thom's Creek, the stream next below Congaree Creek, and about twelve miles below the city. Here the Confederate troops, consisting of the mounted men of Hampton, Wheeler, Butler, &c., made stubborn head against Sherman, holding him in check by constant skirmishing. This skirmishing continued throughout Wednesday, but failed to arrest his progress; and as the Federal cannon continued momently to sound more heavily upon our ears, we were but too certainly assured of the hopelessness of the struggle. The odds of force against the Confederates were too vast for any valor or generalship to make head against it; and yet, almost to this moment, the hope was held out to the people, in many quarters, that the city would be saved. It was asserted that the corps of Cheatham and Stewart were making forced marches, with the view to a junction with the troops under Beauregard, and, such was the spirit of the Confederate troops, and one of the Generals at least, that almost at the moment when Sherman's advance was entering the town, Hampton's cavalry was in order of battle, and only waiting the command to charge it. But the horrors of a street fight in a defenceless city, filled with women and children, were prudently avoided; and the Confederate troops were drawn off from the scene at the very hour when the Federals were entering upon it. But we anticipate.

CHAPTER VII.

THE BOMBARDMENT OF COLUMBIA—THE CITY UNDER MARTIAL LAW—WANT OF TRANSPORTATION—ROBBERIES.

Whatever hopes might have been entertained of the ultimate success of our defences, they were all dissipated, when, by daylight, on the 16th, (Thursday,) the Confederate troops re-entered the city, burning the several bridges over the Congaree, the Broad and Saluda Rivers. They were quartered through the day about the streets, and along their several bivouacs they dug slight excavations in the earth, as for rifle pits and for protection from the shells, which fell fast and thick about the town. The shelling commenced the evening before, and continued throughout the night and the next day. No summons for surrender had been made; no warning of any kind was given. New batteries were in rapid progress of erection on the West side of the Congaree, the more effectually to press the work of destruction. The damage was comparatively slight. The new capitol building was struck five times, but suffered little or no injury. Numerous shells fell into the inhabited portions of the town, yet we hear of only two persons killed—one on the hospital square, and another near the South Carolina Railroad Depot. The venerable Mr. S. J. Wagner, from Charleston, an aged citizen of near eighty, narrowly escaped with life, a shell bursting at his feet. His face was excoriated by the fragments, and for awhile his eye-sight was lost; but we are happy to state that the hurts were slight, and he is now as well as ever.

On Wednesday, the 15th, the city was placed under martial law, and the authority confided to General E. M. Law, assisted by Mayor Goodwyn and Captains W. B. Stanley and John McKenzie. With characteristic energy, the officer executed his trusts, and was employed day and night in the maintenance of order. This, with some few exceptions, was surprisingly maintained. There was some riotous conduct after night. Some highway robberies were committed, and several stores broken open and robbed. But, beyond these, there were but few instances of crime and insubordination.

Terrible, meanwhile, was the press, the shock, the rush, the hurry, the universal confusion—such as might naturally be looked for, in the circumstances of a city from which thousands were preparing to fly, without previous preparations for flight—burdened with pale and trembling women, their children and portable chattels—trunks and jewels, family Bibles and the *lares familiares*. The railroad depot for Charlotte was crowded with anxious waiters upon the train—with a wilderness of luggage—millions, perhaps, in value—much of which was left finally and lost. Throughout Tuesday, Wednesday, and Thursday, these scenes of struggle were in constant performance. The citizens fared badly. The Governments of the State and of the Confederacy absorbed all the modes of conveyance. Transportation about the city could not be had, save by a rich or favored few. No love could pursuade where money failed to convince, and SELF, growing bloated in its dimensions, stared one from every hurrying aspect, as you traversed the excited and crowded streets. In numerous instances, those who succeeded in getting away, did so at the cost of trunks and luggage; and, under what discomfort they departed, no one who did not see can radily conceive.

CHAPTER VIII.

EVACUATION OF COLUMBIA BY THE CONFEDERATE TROOPS— TERRIBLE EXPLOSION AT THE SOUTH CAROLINA RAILROAD DEPOT—THE COMMISSARY AND QUARTERMASTER STORES THROWN OPEN—THE SURRENDER OF THE CITY BY THE MAYOR—THE MAYOR'S LETTER—ASSURANCES OF PROTECTION BY THE FEDERAL OFFICERS.

The end was rapidly approaching. The guns were resounding at the gates. Defence was impossible. At a late hour on Thursday night, the Governor, with his suite and a large train of officials, departed. The Confederate army began its evacuation, and by daylight few remained who were not resigned to the necessity of seeing the tragedy played out. After all the depletion, the city contained, according to our estimate, at least twenty thousand inhabitants, the larger proportion being females and children and negroes. Hampton's cavalry, as we have already mentioned, lingered till near 10 o'clock the next day, and scattered groups of Wheeler's command hovered about the Federal army at their entrance into the town.

The inhabitants were startled at daylight, on Friday morning, by a heavy explosion. This was the South Carolina Railroad Depot. It was accidentally blown up. Broken open by a band of plunderers, among whom were many females and negroes, their reckless greed precipitated their fate. This building had been made the receptacle of supplies from sundry quarters, and was crowded with stores of merchants and planters, trunks of treasure, innumerable wares and goods of fugitives—all of great value. It appears that, among its contents, were some kegs of powder. The plunderers paid, and suddenly, the penalties of their crime. Using their lights freely and hurriedly, the better to *pick*, they fired a train of powder leading to the kegs. The explosion followed, and the number of persons destroyed is variously estimated, from seventeen to fifty. It is probable that not more than thirty-five suffered, but the actual number perishing is unascertained.

At an early hour on Friday, the commissary and quartermaster stores were thrown wide, the contents cast out into the streets and given to the people. The negroes especially loaded themselves with plunder. All this might have been saved, had the officers been duly warned by the military authorities of the probable issue of the struggle. Wheeler's cavalry also shared largely of this plunder, and several of them might be seen, bearing off huge bales upon their saddles.

It was proposed that the white flag should be displayed from the tower of the City Hall. But General Hampton, whose command had not yet left the city, and who was still eager to do battle in its defence, indignantly declared that if displayed, he should have it torn down.

The following letter from the Mayor to General Sherman was the initiation of the surrender:

MAYOR'S OFFICE
COLUMBIA, S. C., February 17, 1865.

To MAJOR-GENERAL SHERMAN: The Confederate forces having evacuated Columbia, I deem it my duty, as Mayor and representative of the city, to ask for its citizens the treatment accorded by the usages of civilized warfare. I therefore respectfully request that you will send a sufficient guard in advance of the army, to maintain order in the city and protect the persons and property of the citizens.

Very respectfully, your obedient servant,

T. J. GOODWYN, Mayor.

At 9 o'clock, on the painfully memorable morning of the 17th February, (Friday,) a deputation from the City Council, consisting of the Mayor, Aldermen McKenzie, Bates and Stork, in a carriage bearing a white flag, proceeded towards the Broad River Bridge Road. Arriving at the forks of the Winnsboro Road, they discovered that the Confederate skirmishers were still busy with their guns, playing upon the advance of the Federals. These were troops of General Wheeler. This conflict was continued simply to afford the main army all possible advantages of a start in their retreat. General Wheeler apprised the deputation that his men would now be withdrawn, and instructed them in what manner to proceed. The deputation met the column of the Federals, under Captain Platt, who sent them forward to Colonel Stone, who finally took his seat with them in the carriage. The advance belonged to the 15th corps.

The Mayor reports that on surrendering the city to Colonel Stone, the latter assured him of the safety of the citzens and of the protection of their property, *while under his command.* He could not answer for General Sherman, who was in the rear, but he expressed the conviction that he would fully confirm the assurances which he (Colonel Stone) had given. Subsequently, General Sherman did confirm them, and that night, seeing that the Mayor was exhausted by his labors of the day, he counselled him to retire to rest, saying, "Not a finger's breadth, Mr. Mayor, of your city shall be harmed. You may lie down to sleep, satisfied that your town shall be as safe in my hands as if wholly in your own." Such was very nearly the language in which he spoke; such was the substance of it. He added: "It will become my duty to destroy some of the public or Government buildings: but I will reserve this performance to another day. It shall be done to-morrow, provided the day be calm." And the Mayor retired with this solemnly asserted and repeated assurance.

CHAPTER IX.

OCCUPATION OF COLUMBIA BY THE FEDERAL ARMY—THE ADVANCE GUARD FIRED UPON—PLUNDERING PRIVATE PROPERTY—THE JAIL FIRED—BURNING COTTON—THE "RAID" ON WATCHES—THE CONVENT—CLERGYMEN ABUSED BY THE SOLDIERS.

About 11 o'clock, the head of the column, following the deputation—the flag of the United States surmounting the carriage—

reached Market Hall, on Main street, while that of the corps was carried in the rear. On their way to the city, the carriage was stopped, and the officer was informed that a large body of Confederate cavalry was flanking them. Colonel Stone said to the Mayor, "We shall hold you responsible for this." The Mayor explained, that the road leading to Winnsboro, by which the Confederates were retreating, ran nearly parallel for a short distance with the river road, which accounted for the apparent flanking. Two officers, who arrived in Columbia ahead of the deputation, (having crossed the river at a point directly opposite the city,) were fired upon by one of Wheeler's cavalry. We are particular in mentioning this fact, as we learn that, subsequently, the incident was urged as a justification of the sack and burning of the city.

Hardly had the troops reached the head of Main street, when the work of pillage was begun. Stores were broken open within the first hour after their arrival, and gold, silver, jewels and liquors, eagerly sought. The authorities, officers, soldiers, all, seemed to consider it a matter of course. And woe to him who carried a watch with gold chain pendant; or who wore a choice hat, or overcoat, or boots or shoes. He was stripped in the twinkling of an eye. It is computed that, from first to last, twelve hundred watches were transferred from the pockets of their owners to those of the soldiers. Purses shared the same fate; nor was the Confederate currency repudiated. But of all these things hereafter, in more detail.

At about 12 o'clock, the jail was discovered to be on fire from within. This building was immediately in rear of the Market, or City Hall, and in a densely built portion of the city. The supposition is that it was fired by some of the prisoners—all of whom were released and subsequently followed the army. The fire of the jail had been preceded by that of some cotton piled in the streets. Both fires were soon subdued by the firemen. At about half-past 1 P. M., that of the jail was rekindled, and was again extinguished. Some of the prisoners, who had been confined at the Asylum, had made their escape, in some instances, a few days before, and were secreted and protected by citizens.

No one felt safe in his own dwelling; and, in the faith that General Sherman would respect the Convent, and have it properly guarded, numbers of young ladies were confided to the care of the Mother Superior, and even trunks of clothes and treasure were sent thither, in full confidence that they would find safety. Vain illusions! The Irish Catholic troops, it appears, were not brought into the city at all; were kept on the other side of the river. But a few Catholics were collected among the corps which occupied the city, and of the conduct of these, a favorable account is given. One of them rescued a silver goblet of the church, used as a drinking cup by a soldier, and restored it to the Rev. Dr. O'Connell. This priest, by the way, was severely handled by the soldiers. Such, also, was the fortune of the Rev. Mr. Shand, of Trinity (the Episcopal) Church, who sought in vain to save a trunk containing the sacred vessels of his church. It was violently wrested from his keeping, and his struggle to save it only provoked the rougher usage. We are since told that, on reaching Camden, General Sherman restored what he believed were these vessels to Bishop Davis. It has since been discovered that the plate belonged to St. Peter's Church in Charleston.

And here it may be well to mention, as suggestive of many clues, an incident which presented a sad commentary on that confidence in the security of the Convent, which was entertained by the great portion of the people. This establishment, under the charge of the sister of the Right Rev. Bishop Lynch, was at once a convent and an academy of the highest class. Hither were sent for education the daughters of Protestants, of the most wealthy classes throughout the State; and these, with the nuns and those young ladies sent thither on the emergency, probably exceeded one hundred. The Lady Superior herself entertained the fullest confidence in the immunities of the establishment. But her confidence was clouded, after she had enjoyed a conference with a certain major of the Yankee army, who described himself as an editor, from Detroit. He visited her at an early hour in the day, and announced his friendly sympathies with the Lady Superior and the sisterhood; professed his anxiety for their safety—his purpose to do all that he could to insure it—declared that he would instantly go to Sherman and secure a chosen guard; and, altogether, made such professions of love and service, as to disarm those suspicions, which his bad looks and bad manners, inflated speech and pompous carriage, might otherwise have provoked. The Lady Superior with such a charge in her hands, was naturally glad to welcome all shows and prospects of support, and expressed her gratitude. He disappeared, and soon after re-appeared, bringing with him no less than eight or ten men—none of them, as he admitted, being Catholics. He had some specious argument to show that, perhaps, her guard had better be one of Protestants. This suggestion staggered the lady a little, but he seemed to convey a more potent reason, when he added, in a whisper: *"For I must tell you, my sister, that Columbia is a doomed city!"* Terrible doom! This officer, leaving his men behind him, disappeared, to show himself no more. The guards so left behind were finally among the most busy as plunderers. The moment that the inmates, driven out by the fire, were forced to abandon their house, they began to revel in its contents.[3]

Quis custodiet ipsos custodes?—who shall guard the guards?— asks the proverb. In a number of cases, the guards provided for the citizens were among the most active plunderers; were quick to betray their trusts, abandon their posts, and bring their comrades in to join in the general pillage. The most dextrous and adroit of these, it is the opinion of most persons, were chiefly Eastern men, or men of immediate Eastern origin.[a] The Western men, including the Indiana, a partion of the Illinois and Iowa, were neither so dextrous nor unscrupulous—were frequently faithful and respectful; and, perhaps, it would be safe to assert that many of the houses which escaped the sack and fire, owed their safety to the presence or the contiguity of some of these men. But we must retrace our steps.

CHAPTER X.

FIRING THE CITY BY SHERMAN'S TROOPS—THE DISCIPLINE OF THE MEN—CITIZENS APPLYING FOR A GUARD—"A REIGN OF TERROR"—THE FIREMEN INTERRUPTED—A TERRIBLE SIGHT —SOLDIERS BURNT TO DEATH—THE CITY CLOCK GIVES ITS LAST SOUND.

---

[3] The Mother Superior of the Ursuline Convent had been a college friend of Sherman's wife. She appealed to Sherman for a guard and he sent the sort of men here described. (*South Carolina Women of the Confederacy*, 1903, 298-301.)

[a] This gives support to the statements made in pages x, xi, xii of the Introduction respecting the propaganda of hate of South Carolina that so early developed in Puritan New England.

It may be well to remark that the discipline of the soldiers, upon their first entry into the city, was perfect and most admirable. There was no disorder or irregularity on the line of march, showing that their officers had them completely in hand. They were a fine looking body of men, mostly young and of vigorous formation, well clad and well shod, seemingly wanting in nothing. Their arms and accoutrements were in bright order. The negroes accompanying them were not numerous, and seemed mostly to act as drudges and body servants. They groomed horses, waited, carried burdens, and, in almost every instance under our eyes, appeared in a purely servile, and not a military, capacity. The men of the West treated them generally with scorn or indifference, sometimes harshly, and not unfrequently with blows.

But, if the entrance into town and while on duty, was indicative of admirable drill and discipline, such ceased to be the case the moment the troops were dismissed. Then, whether by tacit permission or direct command, their whole deportment underwent a sudden and rapid change. The saturnalia soon began. We have shown that the robbery of the persons of the citizens and the plunder of their homes commenced within one hour after they had reached the Market Hall. It continued without interruption throughout the day. Sherman, at the head of his cavalry, traversed the streets everywhere—so did his officers. Subsequently, these officers were everywhere on foot, yet beheld nothing which required the interposition of authority. And yet robbery was going on at every corner—in nearly every house. Citizens generally applied for a guard at their several houses, and, for a time, these guards were allotted them. These might be faithful or not. In some cases, as already stated, they were, and civil and respectful; considerate of the claims of women, and never trespassing upon the privacy of the family; but, in numbers of cases, they were intrusive, insulting and treacherous —leaving no privacy undisturbed, passing without a word into the chambers and prying into every crevice and corner.

But the reign of terror did not fairly begin till night. In some instances, where parties complained of the misrule and robbery, their guards said to them, with a chuckle: "This is nothing. Wait till to-night, and you'll see h—ll."

Among the first fires at evening was one about dark, which

broke out in a filthy purlieu of low houses, of wood, on Gervais street, occupied mostly as brothels. Almost at the same time, a body of the soldiers scattered over the Eastern outskirts of the city, fired severally the dwellings of Mr. Secretary Trenholm, General Wade Hampton, Dr. John Wallace, J. U. Adams, Mrs. Starke, Mr. Latta, Mrs. English, and many others. There were then some twenty fires in full blast, in as many different quarters, and while the alarm sounded from these quarters a similar alarm was sent up almost simultaneously from Cotton Town, the Northermost limit of the city, and from Main street in its very centre, at the several stores or houses of O. Z. Bates, C. D. Eberhardt, and some others, in the heart of the most densely settled portion of the town; thus enveloping in flames almost every section of the devoted city. At this period, thus early in the evening, there were few shows of that drunkenness which prevailed at a late hour in the night, and only after all the grocery shops on Main street had been rifled. The men engaged in this were well prepared with all the appliances essential to their work. They did not need the torch. They carried with them, from house to house, pots and vessels containing combustible liquids, composed probably of phosphorous and other similar agents, turpentine, &c.; and, with balls of cotton saturated in this liquid, with which they also overspread floors and walls, they conveyed the flames with wonderful rapidity from dwelling to dwelling. Each had his ready box of Lucifer matches, and, with a scrape upon the walls, the flames began to rage. Where houses were closely contiguous, a brand from one was the means of conveying destruction to the other.

The winds favored. They had been high throughout the day, and steadily prevailed from South-west by West, and bore the flames Eastward. To this fact we owe the preservation of the portions of the city lying West of Assembly street.

The work, begun thus vigorously, went on without impediment and with hourly increase throughout the night. Engines and hose were brought out by the firemen, but these were soon driven from their labors—which were indeed idle against such a storm of fire—by the pertinacious hostility of the soldiers; the hose was hewn to pieces, and the firemen, dreading worse usage to themselves, left the field in despair. Meanwhile, the flames spread from side to side, from front to rear, from street to street, and where their natural and inevitable progress was too slow for those who had kindled them, they helped them on by the application of fresh combustibles and more rapid agencies of conflagration. By midnight, Main street, from its Northern to its Southern extremity, was a solid wall of fire. By 12 o'clock, the great blocks, which included the banking houses and the Treasury buildings, were consumed; Janney's (Congaree) and Nickerson's Hotels; the magnificent manufactories of Evans & Cogswell—indeed every large block in the business portion of the city; the old Capitol and all the adjacent buildings were in ruins. The range called the "Granite" was beginning to flame at 12, and might have been saved by ten vigorous men, resolutely working.

At 1 o'clock, the hour was struck by the clock of the Market Hall, which was even then illuminated from within. It was its own last hour which it sounded, and its tongue was silenced forevermore. In less than five minutes after, its spire went down with a crash, and, by this time, almost all the buildings within the precinct were a mass of ruins.

Very grand, and terrible, beyond description, was the awful spectacle. It was a scene for the painter of the terrible. It was the blending of a range of burning mountains stretched in a continuous series of more than a mile. Here was Ætna, sending up its spouts of flaming lava; Vesuvius, emulous of like display, shooting up with loftier torrents, and Stromboli, struggling, with awful throes, to shame both by its superior volumes of fluid flame. The winds were tributary to these convulsive efforts, and tossed the volcanic torrents of sulphurous cloud— wreaths of sable, edged with sheeted lightnings, wrapped the skies, and, at short intervals, the falling tower and the tottering wall, avalanche-like, went down with thunderous sound, sending up at every crash great billowy showers of glowing fiery embers.

Throughout the whole of this terrible scene the soldiers continued their search after spoil. The houses were severally and soon gutted of their contents. Hundreds of iron safes, warranted "impenetrable to fire and the burglar," it was soon satisfactorily demonstrated, were not "Yankee proof." They were split open and robbed, yielding, in some cases, very largely of Confederate money and bonds, if not of gold and silver. Jewelry and plate in abundance was found. Men could be seen staggering off with huge waiters, vases, candelabra, to say nothing of cups, goblets and smaller vessels, all of solid silver. Clothes and shoes, when new, were appropriated—the rest left to burn. Liquors were drank with such avidity as to astonish the veteran Bacchanals of Columbia; nor did the parties thus distinguishing themselves hesitate about the vintage. There was no idle discrimination in the matter of taste, from that vulgar liquor, which Judge Burke used to say always provoked within him "an inordinate propensity to sthale," to the choiciest red wines of the ancient cellars. In one vault on Main street, seventeen casks of wine were stored away, which, an eye-witness tells us, barely sufficed, once broken into, for the draughts of a single hour—such were the appetites at work and the numbers in possession of them. Rye, corn, claret and Madeira all found their way into the same channels, and we are not to wonder, when told that no less than one hundred and fifty of the drunken creatures perished miserably among the flames kindled by their own comrades, and from which they were unable to escape. The estimate will not be thought extravagant by those who saw the condition of hundreds after 1 o'clock A. M. By others, however, the estimate is reduced to thirty; but the number will never be known. Sherman's officers themselves are reported to have said that they lost more men in the sack and burning of the city (including certain explosions) than in all their fights while approaching it. It is also suggested that the orders which Sherman issued at daylight, on Saturday morning, for the arrest of the fire, were issued in consequence of the loss of men which he had thus sustained.

One or more of his men were shot, by parties unknown, in some dark passages or alleys—it is supposed in consequence of some attempted outrages which humanity could not endure; the assassin taking advantage of the obscurity of the situation and adroitly mingling with the crowd without. And while these scenes were at their worst—while the flames were at their highest and most extensively raging—groups might be seen at the several corners of the streets, drinking, roaring, revelling—while the fiddle and accordeon were playing their popular airs among them. There was no cessation of the work till 5 A. M. on Saturday.

CHAPTER XI.

UNSUCCESSFUL ATTEMPTS TO SAVE PROPERTY—FEMALES ILL-
TREATED—A GUARD PERFORMS HIS DUTY—A PLUCKY CIT-
IZEN—FAMILIES QUARTERED IN THE STREETS—A COOL PRO-
CEEDING—"A BIG DRUNK."

A single thought will suffice to show that the owners or lodg-
ers in the houses thus sacrificed were not silent or quiet spectators of a conflagration which threw them naked and homeless
under the skies of night. The male population, consisting mostly of aged men, invalids, decrepits, women and children, were
not capable of very active or powerful exertions; but they did
not succumb to the fate without earnest pleas and strenuous efforts. Old men and women and children were to be seen, even
while the flames were rolling and raging around them, while
walls were crackling and rafters tottering and tumbling, in the
endeavor to save their clothing and some of their most valuable
effects. It was not often that they were suffered to succeed.
They were driven out headlong.

Ladies were hustled from their chambers—their ornaments
plucked from their persons, their bundles from their hands. It
was in vain that the mother appealed for the garments of her
children. They were torn from her grasp and hurled into the
flames. The young girl striving to save a single frock, had it
rent to fibres in her grasp. Men and women bearing off their
trunks were seized, despoiled, in a moment the trunk burst asun-
der with the stroke of axe or gun-butt, the contents laid bare,
rifled of all the objects of desire, and the residue sacrificed to
the fire. You might see the ruined owner, standing woe-begone,
aghast, gazing at his tumbling dwelling, his scattered property,
with a dumb agony in his face that was inexpressibly touching.
Others you might hear, as we did, with wild blasphemies assail-
ing the justice of Heaven, or invoking, with lifted and clenched
hands, the fiery wrath of the avenger. But the soldiers plundered and drank, the fiery work raged, and the moon sailed
over all with as serene an aspect as when she first smiled upon
the ark resting against the slopes of Ararat.

Such was the spectacle for hours on the chief business street
of Columbia.

We have intimated that, at an early hour in the day, almost every house was visited by groups, averaging in number from two to six persons. Some of these entered civilly enough, but pertinaciously entered, in some cases, *begging* for milk, eggs, bread and meat—in most cases, demanding them. The kitchens were entered frequently by one party, while another penetrated the dwelling, and the cook was frequently astounded by the audacity by which the turkey, duck, fowl or roast was transferred from the spit to the wallet of the soldier. In the house, parties less meek of temper than these pushed their way, and the first intimation of their presence, as they were confronted at the entrance, was a pistol clapped at the head or bosom of the owner, whether male or female.

"Your watch!" "Your money!" was the demand. Frequently, no demand was made. Rarely, indeed, was a word spoken, where the watch or chain, or ring or bracelet, presented itself conspicuously to the eye. It was incontinently plucked away from the neck, breast or bosom. Hundreds of women, still greater numbers of old men, were thus despoiled. The slightest show of resistance provoked violence to the person.

The venerable Mr. Alfred Huger was thus robbed in the chamber and presence of his family, and in the eye of an almost dying wife. He offered resistance, and was collared and dispossessed by violence.

We are told that the venerable ex-Senator, Colonel Arthur P. Hayne, was treated even more roughly.

Mr. James Rose, besides his watch, lost largely of choice wines, which had been confided to his keeping.

But we cannot descend to examples. In the open streets the pickpockets were mostly active. A frequent mode of operating was by first asking you the hour. If thoughtless enough to reply, producing the watch or indicating its possession, it was quietly taken from hand or pocket, and transferred to the pocket of the "other gentleman," with some such remark as this: "A pretty little watch that. I'll take it myself; it just suits me." And the appropriation followed; and if you hinted any dislike to the proceeding, a grasp was taken of your collar and the muzzle of a revolver put to your ear. Some of the incidents connected with this wholesale system were rather amusing.

Dr. Templeton, a well known and highly esteemed citizen, passing along the street, was accosted by a couple of these experts, who stopped and asked him, pointing to the arsenal building, on the hill opposite, "What building is that?"

"The State Arsenal," was his reply, unwisely extending his arm, as he pointed, in turn, to the building, and revealing between the folds of his coat the shining links of a rich gold chain.

Before he could recover himself, his chain and watch were in the grasp of the thief, who was preparing to transfer it to his own pocket, quietly remarking, " A very pretty little watch; just to my liking."

"That is very cool," said Templeton.

"Just my way," said the fellow, walking off.

"Stop," said Templeton, half amazed at the coolness of the proceeding, and feeling that he had only to put the best face on the matter. "Stop; that watch will be of no use to you without the key; won't you take that also?"

"All right," replied the robber, returning and receiving the key.

The question, "What's o'clock," was the sure forerunner of an attempt upon your pocket. Some parties saved their chronometers by an adroitness which deserves to be made known. One individual replied to the question: "You are too late my good fellows. I was asked that question already by one of your parties, at the other corner." He left them to infer that the watch was already gone, and they passed him by.

We are told of one person who, being thus asked for the time of day by three of them, in a street in which he could see no other of their comrades, thrust a revolver suddenly into their faces, and cocking it quickly, cried out, "Look for yourselves." They sheered off and left him.

We, ourselves, were twice asked the question the morning after the fire, and looking innocently to where the City Hall clock once stood, replied, "Our city clock is gone, you see; but it must be near 11."

Mr. J. K. Robinson was assailed with the same question by

a party in the neighborhood of his house.   He denied that he had a watch.

"Oh! look, look!" was the answer of the questioner.

"I need not look," quoth Robinson, "since I have not a watch."

"Look, look—a man of your appearance *must* own a watch."

"Well, I do; but it is at my home—at my house."

"Where's your house? We'll go and see."

He took them into his house, suddenly called his guard and said, "These men are pursuing me; I know not what they want."

The guard drove out the party, with successive thrusts at them of the bayonet, and from the street, defrauded of their spoils, they saluted house guard and owner with all manner of horrid execrations.

Hundreds of like anecdotes are told, not merely of loss in watches, but of every other article of property. Hats and boots, overcoats and shawls—these, when new and attractive, were sure to be taken. Even the negroes were despoiled, whenever the commodity was of any value.

An incident occurred, which, though amusing to read of, could not have been very pleasant to one of the party engaged at least. A gentleman was directed to break in the heads and empty the contents of some forty barrels of whiskey stored at the Fair Grounds. He had proceeded with the job only so far as breaking in the heads of the barrels, when a number of soldiers entered the building, and stopped all further proceeding. They charged him with poisoning the liquor, and forced him to take a drink from every barrel, before they would touch the contents. The consequence was, that he was drunk for over a week.

CHAPTER XII.

SCENES AND INCIDENTS—THE SOLDIERS AND THE LADIES— "PLUCK" OF THE SOUTH CAROLINA LADIES—THE POOR FRENCH LADY WITH THE SOLDIERS—WHAT OCCURRED IN THE HOUSES—"SWAPPING" GUNS—AN OFFICER PROTECTS A HOUSE—SINGULAR INCIDENT.

Within the dwellings, the scenes were of more harsh and

tragical character, rarely softened by any ludicrous aspects, as they were screened by the privacy of the apartment, with but few eyes to witness. The pistol to the bosom or the head of woman, the patient mother, the trembling daughter, was the ordinary introduction to the demand. "Your gold, silver, watch, jewels." They gave no time, allowed no pause or hesitation. It was in vain that the woman offered her keys, or proceeded to open drawer, or wardrobe, or cabinet, or trunk. It was dashed to pieces by axe or gun-butt, with the cry, "We have a shorter way than that!" It was in vain that she pleaded to spare her furniture, and she would give up all its contents.

All the precious things of a family, such as the heart loves to pore on in quiet hours when alone with memory—the dear miniature, the photograph, the portrait—these were dashed to pieces, crushed under foot, and the more the trembler pleaded for the object so precious, the more violent the rage which destroyed it. Nothing was sacred in their eyes, save the gold and silver which they bore away. Nor were these acts those of common soldiers. Commissioned officers, of rank so high as that of a colonel, were frequently among the most active in spoliation, and not always the most tender or considerate in the manner and acting of their crimes. And, after glutting themselves with spoil, would often utter the foulest speeches, coupled with oaths as condiment, dealing in what they assumed, besides, to be bitter sarcasms upon the cause and country.

"And what do you think of the Yankees now?" was a frequent question. "Do you not fear us, now," "What do you think of secession?" &c., &c. "We mean to wipe you out! We'll burn the very stones of South Carolina." Even General Howard, who is said to have been once a pious parson, is reported to have made this reply to a citizen who had expostulated with him on the monstrous crime of which his army had been guilty: "It is only what the country deserves. It is her fit punishment; and if this does not quiet rebellion, and we have to return, we will do this work thoroughly. We will not leave woman or child.[4]

---

4 Men of the intelligence of General Howard did not believe the Southern States were engaged in rebellion. They knew that they themselves were engaged in a war of conquest, which was but a more vigorous method of robbing the Southern States of their political and property rights than had been practiced theretofore. Rebellion was a term that enabled many cowards to vent the pent up hatred that had rankled in their blood and that of their ancestors for nearly two centuries.

Almost universally, the women of Columbia behaved themselves nobly under their insults. They preserved that patient, calm demeanor, that simple, almost masculine firmness, which so becomes humanity in the hour of trial, when nothing can be opposed to the tempest but the virtue of inflexible endurance. They rarely replied to these insults; but looking coldly into the faces of the assailants, heard them in silence and with unblenching cheeks. When forced to answer, they did so in monosyllables only, or in brief, stern language, avowed their confidence in the cause of their country, the principles and rights for which their brothers and sons fought, and their faith in the ultimate favor and protection of God. One or two of many of these dialogues— if they may be called such, where one of the parties can urge his speech with all the agencies of power for its enforcement, and with all his instruments of terror in sight, while the other stands exposed to the worst terrors which maddened passions, insolent in the consciousness of strength—may suffice as a sample of many:

"Well, what do you think of the Yankees now?"

"Do you expect a favorable opinion?"

"No! d—n it! But you fear us, and that's enough."

"No—we do not fear you."

"What! not yet?"

"Not yet!"

"But you shall fear us."

"Never!"

"We'll make you."

"You may inflict, we can endure; but fear—never! Anything but that."

In 1867 General Howard came to Columbia in connection with that contemptible fraud designated "the Freedman's Bureau". While in Governor Orr's office—there being present besides the Governor and General Howard, Gen. John S. Preston, Col. James G. Gibbes and F. G. deFontaine —General Hampton came in. Someone offered to introduce Hampton to Howard. Colonel Gibbes once told the writer that General Hampton drew himself up and said: "Before I take your hand General Howard tell me who burnt Columbia." Howard's reply was: "It is useless to deny that our troops burnt Columbia, for I saw them in the act." (See Edwin J. Scott, *Random Recollections of a Long Life*, 185; *The Burning of Columbia*, Charleston, S. C., 1888, 11.)

"We'll make you fear us!" clapping a revolver to the lady's head.

Her eye never faltered. Her cheek never changed its color. Her lips were firmly compressed. Her arms folded on her bosom. The eye of the assassin glared into her own. She met the encounter without flinching, and he lowered the implement of murder, with an oath: "D—n it! You have pluck enough for a whole regiment!"

In a great many cases the guard behaved themselves well, using their utmost endeavors to protect the property under their charge, even to the use of the bayonet.

An officer, Lieutenant McQueen, stopped with Dr. Wm. Reynolds, and during the fire, worked manfully, and was the means of saving the residence from destruction. His gentlemanly manners won the respect and confidence of the family, and when he was on the point of leaving, the doctor gave him a letter, signed by several gentlemen, acknowledging his grateful feelings for the manner in which he had been treated; saying that the fortunes of war might some time place him in a position that the letter might be of use to him. This proved to be the case. At the skirmish near Lynch's Creek, this officer was wounded and captured.[a] On showing the letter to a friend of Dr. Reynolds, who happened to be in the hospital, he was removed to a private house, every attention shown him, and when he was able to move, a special parole was obtained for him, and he returned to his home.

The "pluck" of our women was especially a subject of acknowledgment. They could admire a quality with which they had not soul to sympathize—or rather the paramount passion for greed and plunder kept in subjection all other qualities, without absolutely extinguishing them from their minds and thoughts. To inspire terror in the weak, strange to say, seemed to them a sort of heroism. To extort fear and awe appeared to their inordinate vanity a tribute more grateful than any other, and a curious conflict was sometimes carried on in their minds between their vanity and cupidity. Occasionally they gave with one hand, while they robbed with another.

Several curious instances of this nature took place, one of

---

[a] By the 5th Regiment, Cavalry, S.C.V., under Captain Zimmerman Davis.

which must suffice. A certain Yankee officer happened to hear that an old acquaintance of his, whom he had known intimately at West Point and Louisiana, was residing in Columbia. He went to see him after the fire, and ascertained that his losses had been very heavy, exceeding two hundred thousand dollars. The parties had not separated for an hour, when a messenger came from the Yankee, bringing a box; which contained one hundred thousand dollars in Confederate notes. This the Yankee begged his Southern friend to accept, as helping to make up his losses. The latter declined the gift, not being altogether satisfied in conscience with regard to it. In many cases, Confederate money by the handfull was bestowed by the officers and soldiers upon parties from whom they had robbed the last particles of clothing, and even General Sherman could give to parties, whom he knew, the flour and bacon which had been taken from starving widows and orphans. So he left with the people of Columbia a hundred old muskets for their protection, while emptying their arsenals of a choice collection of beautiful Enfield rifles. And so the starving citizens of Columbia owe to him a few hundred starving cattle, which he had taken from the starving people of Beaufort, Barnwell, Orangeburg and Lexington—cattle left without food, and for which food could not be found, and dying of exhaustion at the rate of fifteen to twenty head per diem.

In this connection and this section, in which we need to devote so much of our space to the cruel treatment of our women, we think it proper to include a communication from the venerable Dr. Sill, one of the most esteemed and well-known citizens of Columbia. It is from his own pen, and the facts occurred under his own eyes. We give this as one of a thousand like cases, witnessed by a thousand eyes, and taking place at the same time in every quarter of the city, almost from the hour of the arrival of the army to that of its departure. He writes as follows:

"On Thursday, the day before the evacuation of the city by the Confederate forces, I invited a very poor French lady, (Madame Pelletier,) with her child, refugees from Charleston, to take shelter in my house, where they might, at least, have such protection as I could give her, shelter and food for herself and child. She was poor, indeed, having very little clothing, and only one or two implements—a sewing machine and a crimping apparatus—by means of which she obtained a precarious support. My own family (happily) and servants being all absent, and being myself wholly incapacitated by years of sickness from making any exertion, all that the poor widow woman and myself could remove from my house, besides the few things of hers, consisted of two bags of flour, a peck of meal, and about the same of grist, and about thirty pounds of bacon and a little sugar. These few things we managed to get out of the house, and, by the aid of a wheelbarrow, removed about fifty yards from the burning buildings. Waiting then and there, waiting anxiously the progress and direction of the fire, we soon found that we had been robbed of one bag of flour and a trunk of valuable books of account and papers. The fire continuing to advance on us, we found it necessary to remove again. About this time, there came up a stalwart soldier, about six feet high, accoutred with pistols, Bowie-knife, &c., and stooping down over the remaining bag of flour, demanded of the poor French lady what the bag contained. Having lost, but a few moments before, almost everything she had in the way of provisions, she seemed most deeply and keenly alive to her destitute situation, in the event she should lose the remaining bag of flour; the last and only hope of escape from starvation of her child and herself. She fell upon her knees, with hands uplifted, in a supplicating manner, and most piteously and imploringly set forth her situation —an appeal which, under the circumstances, it would be impossible to conceive, more touching or heart-rending. She told him she was not here of her own choice; that herself and husband had come to Charleston in 1860 to better their fortunes; that they had been domiciled in New Jersey, where her husband had taken the necessary steps to become a citizen of the United States. She had in her hands his papers vouching the truth of her statement; that her husband had died of yellow fever in Charleston; that being unable, from want of the means, to return to New Jersey, she had been driven from Charleston to Columbia, (a refugee, flying from the enemy's shells,) to try to make an honest support for herself and child. To all this, he not only turned a deaf ear, but deliberately drew from his breast a huge shining Bowie-knife, brandished it in her face, rudely pushed her aside, using, at the same time, the most menacing and obscene language; shouldered the bag of flour, and marched off, leaving the poor starving creature, with her helpless child, overwhelmed with grief and despair.   E. SILL."

This is surely very piteous to hear, and were the case an isolated one, it would probably move compassion in every heart; but where the miseries of like and worse sort, of a whole community of twenty thousand, are massed, as it were, together before the eyes, the sensibilities become obtuse, and the universal suffering seems to destroy the sensibilities in all. We shall not seek to multiply instances like the foregoing, which would be an endless work and little profit.

CHAPTER XIII.

GENERAL SHERMAN ON FORAGING

General Sherman tells General Hampton that, could he find any civil authority, and could they provide him with forage and provisions, he would suffer no foraging upon the people.[5] His logic and memory are equally deficient. Was there no Mayor and Council in Columbia? They had formally surrendered the city into his hands. They constituted the civil authority; but he made no requisition upon them for provisions for his troops. He did not say to them, "Supply me with twenty thousand rations in so many hours." Had he done so, the rations would have been forthcoming. The citizens would have been only too glad, by yielding up one-half of their stores, to have saved the other half, and to have preserved their dwellings from the presence of the soldiers. Nay, did not the in-dwellers of every house—we will say five thousand houses—seek at his hands a special guard—which usually consisted of two men—and were not these fed wholly by the families where they lodged during the whole time of their stay? Here, by a very simple computation, we find that ten thousand soldiers were thus voluntarily provided with rations; and a requisition for twenty thousand men might easily and would probably have been provided, had any such been made; for the supplies in the city were abundant of every sort—the population generally having laid in largely, and without stint or limit, anticipating a period of general scarcity from the march of the enemy.

But, even had the people been unable to supply these provis-

---

5 *The Burning of Columbia*, Charleston, 1888, 15, for Sherman's letter to Hampton.

ions—even had the Council failed to respond to these requisitions—at whose doors should the blame be laid? The failure would have been the direct consequences of General Sherman's own proceedings. Had he not ravaged and swept, with a bosom of fire, all the tracts of country upon which the people of Columbia depended for their supplies? Had he not, himself, cut off all means of transportation, in the destruction, not only of the railways, but of every wagon, cart, vehicle, on all the plantations through which he had passed—carrying off all the beasts of burden of any value, and cutting the throats of the remainder? He cuts off the feet and arms of a people, and then demands that they shall bring him food and forage!

But even this pretext, if well grounded, can avail him nothing. He was suffering from no sort of necessity. It was the boast of every officer and soldier in his army, that he had fed fat upon the country through which he had passed; everywhere finding abundance, and had not once felt the necessity of lifting the cover from his own wagons, and feeding from his own accumulated stores. But the complaint of Hampton, and of our people at large, is not that he *fed* his followers upon the country, but that he destroyed what he did not need for food, and tore the bread from the famishing mouths of a hundred thousand women and children—feeble infancy and decrepit age.

CHAPTER XIV.

OUTRAGES ON NEGRO WOMEN—A LADY IN CHILD-BED FRIGHTENED TO DEATH—FATHERS PROTECTING THEIR DAUGHTERS —A NEW USE FOR PARLORS.

We have adverted to the outrages which were perpetrated within the households of the citizen, where, unrestrained by the rebuking eyes of their comrades, and unresisted by their interposition, cupidity, malignity and lust, sought to glut their several appetites. The cupidity generally triumphed over the lust. The greed for gold and silver swallowed up the more animal passions, and drunkenness supervened in season for the safety of many.

We have heard of some few outrages, or attempts at outrage, of the worst sort, but the instances, in the case of white females, must have been very few. There was, perhaps, a wholesome dread of goading to desperation the people whom they had despoiled of all but honor. They could see, in many watchful and guardian eyes, the lurking expression which threatened sharp vengeance, should their tresspasses proceed to those extremes which they yet unquestionably contemplated.

The venerable Mr. H ——— stood ready, with his *couteau de chasse,* made bare in his bosom, hovering around the persons of his innocent daughters. Mr. O.———, on beholding some too familiar approach to one of his daughters bade the man stand off at the peril of his life; saying that while he submitted to be robbed of property, he would sacrifice life without reserve—his own and that of the assailant—before his child's honor should be abused.

Mr. James G. Gibbes, with difficulty, pistol in hand, and only with the assistance of a Yankee officer, rescued two young women from the clutches of as many ruffians.

We have been told of successful outrages of this unmentionable character being practiced upon women dwelling in the suburbs. Many are understood to have taken place in remote country settlements, and two cases are described where young negresses were brutally forced by the wretches and afterwards murdered—one of them being thrust, when half dead, head down, into a mud puddle, and there held until she was suffocated. But this must suffice.

The shocking details should not now be made, but that we need, for the sake of truth and humanity, to put on record the horrid deeds. And yet, we should grossly err if, while showing the forbearance of the soldiers in respect to our *white* women, we should convey to any innocent reader the notion that they exhibited a like forbearance in the case of the *black.* The poor negroes were terribly victimized by their assailants, many of them, besides the instance mentioned, being left in a condition little short of death. Regiments, in successive *relays,* subjected scores of these poor women to the torture of their embraces, and —but we dare not further pursue the subject. There are some horrors which the historian dare not pursue—which the painter dare not delineate. They both drop the curtain over crimes which humanity bleeds to contemplate.

Some incidents of gross brutality, which show how well prepared were these men for every crime, however monstrous, may be given.

A lady, undergoing the pains of labor, had to be borne out on a mattress into the open air, to escape the fire. It was in vain that her situation was described as the soldiers applied the the torch within and without the house, after they had penetrated every chamber and robbed them of all that was either valuable or portable. They beheld the situation of the sufferer, and laughed to scorn the prayer for her safety.

Another lady, Mrs. J——, was but recently confined. Her condition was very helpless. Her life hung upon a hair. The men were apprised of all the facts in the case. They burst into the chamber—took the rings from the lady's fingers—plucked the watch from beneath her pillow, and so overwhelmed her with terror, that she sunk under the treatment—surviving their departure but a day or two.

In several instances, parlors, articles of crockery, and even beds, were used by the soldiers as if they were water closets. In one case, a party used vessels in this way, then put them on the bed, fired at and smashed them to pieces, emptying the filthy contents over the bedding.

In several cases, newly made graves were opened, the coffins taken out, broken open, in search of buried treasure, and the corpses left exposed. Every spot in grave-yard or garden, which seemed to have been recently disturbed, was sounded with sword, or bayonet, or ramrod, in their desperate search after spoil.

CHAPTER XV.

THE DEAD DOG—GENERAL SHERMAN'S ASSURANCE TO THE MAYOR—THE SIGNAL ROCKETS.

In this grave connection, we have to narrate a somewhat picturesque transaction, less harsh of character and less tragic, and preserving a somewhat redeeming aspect to the almost uniform brutality of our foes. Mr. M. M. C.—— had a guard given him for his home, who not only proved faithful to their trust, but showed themselves gentle and unobtrusive. Their comrades, in large numbers, were encamped on the adjoining and vacant lands. These latter penetrated his grounds, breaking their way through the fences, and it was not possible, where there were so many, to prevent their aggression entirely. The guard kept them out of the dwelling, and preserved its contents. They were not merely civil, but amused the children of the family; played with them, sympathized in their fun, and contributed to their little sports in sundry ways. The children owned a pretty little pet, a grey-hound, which was one of the most interesting of their sources of enjoyment. The soldiers, without, seemed to remark this play of the guard with the children and dog with discontent and displeasure. They gave several indications of a morose temper in regard to them, and, no doubt, they considered the guard with hostility, *per se*, as guard, and because of their faithful protection of the family. At length, their displeasure prompted one of them to take an active but cruel part in the pastimes of the children. Gathering up a stone, he watched his moment, and approaching the group, where they were at play, suddenly dashed out the brains of the little dog, at the very feet of the children. They were terribly frightened, of course, at this cruel exhibition of power and malignity. Their grief followed in bitter lamentations and tears. To soothe them, the soldiers of the guard took up the remains of the dog, dug for it a grave in one of the flower beds of the garden, tenderly laid it in the earth, and raised a mound over it, precisely as if it had been a human child. A stake at the head and feet rendered the proceeding complete.

That night, Mr. C——, returning home, his wife remarked to him:

"We have lost our silver. It was buried in the very spot where these men have buried the dog. They have no doubt found it, and it is lost to us."

It was impossible then to attempt any search for the relief of their anxiety, until the departure of the troops. When they had gone, however, the search was eagerly made, and the buried treasure found untouched. But the escape was a narrow one. The cavity made for the body of the dog approached within a few inches the box of silver.

Mayor Goodwyn also saved a portion of his plate through the

fidelity of his guard. But he lost his dwelling and everything besides. We believe that, in every instance where the guard proved faithful, they were Western men. They professed to revolt at the spectacles of crime which they were compelled to witness, and pleaded the necessity of a blind obedience to orders, in justification of their share of the horrors to which they lent their hands. Just before the conflagration began, about the dusk of evening, while the Mayor was conversing with one of the Western men, from Iowa, three rockets were shot up by the enemy from the capitol square. As the soldier beheld these rockets, he cried out:

"Alas! alas! for your poor city! It is doomed. Those rockets are the signal. The town is to be fired."

In less than twenty minutes after, the flames broke out in twenty distinct quarters. Similar statements were made by other soldiers in different quarters of the city.

CHAPTER XVI.

THE STREETS OF THE CITY—THE CHURCHES FIRED—SIDNEY PARK.

Of the conflagration itself, we have already given a sufficient idea, so far as words may serve for the description of a scene which beggars art and language to portray. We have also shown, in some degree, the usual course of proceedure among the soldiers; how they fired the dwelling as they pillaged; how they abused and outraged the in-dwellers; how they mocked at suffering, scorned the pleadings of women and innocence.

As the flames spread from house to house, you could behold, through long vistas of the lurid empire of flames and gloom, the miserable tenants of the once peaceful home issuing forth in dismay, bearing the chattels most useful or precious, and seeking escape through the narrow channels which the flames left them only in the centre of the streets. Fortunately, the streets of Columbia are very wide,[6] and greatly protected by

---

[6] There are eighteen streets and three avenues running north and south and a like number of each running east and west. The streets are one hundred feet wide and the avenues one hundred and fifty feet wide. Two of the avenues intersect at right angles in the centre of the city and the four boundaries are avenues.

umbrageous trees, set in regular order, and which, during the vernal season, confer upon the city one of its most beautiful features. But for this width of its passages, thousands must have been burned to death.

These families moved in long procession, the aged sire or grand-sire first—a sad, worn and tottering man, walking steadily on, with rigid, set features and tearless eyes—too much stricken, too much stunned, for any ordinary shows of suffering. Perhaps, the aged wife hung upon one arm, while the other was supported by a daughter. And huddling close, like terrified partridges, came the young, each bearing some little bundle—all pressing forward under the lead of the sire, and he witless where to go. The ascending fire-spouts flamed before them on every hand—shouts assailed them at every step—the drunken soldiers danced around them as they went, piercing their ears with horrid threats and imprecations. The little bundles were snatched from the grasp of their trembling bearers, torn open, and what was not appropriated, was hurled into the contiguous pile of flame. And group after group, stream after stream of fugitives thus pursued their way through the paths of flaming and howling horror, only too glad to fling themselves on the open ground, whither, in some cases, they had succeeded in conveying a feather bed or mattress. The malls, or open squares, the centres of the wide streets, like Assembly street, were thus strewn with piles of bedding on which lay exhausted mothers—some of them with anxious physicians in attendance, and girded by crouching children and infants, wild and almost idiotic with their terrors. In one case, as we have mentioned, a woman about to become a mother was thus borne out from a burning dwelling.

It was scarcely possible to advise in which direction to fly. The churches were at first sought by many several streams of population. But these were found to afford no security—the churches of God were set on flame. Again driven forth, numbers made their way into the recesses of Sidney Park, and here fancied to find security, as but few houses occupied the neighborhood, and these not sufficiently high to lead to apprehension from the flames. But the fire-balls were thrown from the heights into the deepest hollows of the park, and the wretched fugitives were forced to scatter, finding their way to other places of retreat, and finding none of them secure.

CHAPTER XVII.

THE NUNS LEAVING THE CONVENT—FEDERAL OFFICERS PROTECT THEM—A NIGHT IN A GRAVE-YARD—REV. L. P. O'CONNELL'S STATEMENT.

One of these mournful processions of fugitives was that of the sisterhood of the Convent, the nuns and their pupils. Beguiled to the last moment by the promises and assurances of officers and others in Sherman's army, the Mother Superior had clung to her house to the last possible moment. It was not merely a home, but in some degree a temple, and, to the professors of one church at least, a shrine. It had been chosen, as we have seen, as the place of refuge for many of other churches. Much treasure had been lodged in it for safe keeping, and the Convent had a considerable treasure of its own. It was liberally and largely furnished, not only as a domain, but as an academy of the highest standard. It was complete in all the agencies and material for such an academy, and for the accommodation of perhaps two hundred pupils. Among these agencies for education were no less than seventeen pianos. The harp, the guitar, the globe, the maps, desks, benches, bedding and clothing, were all supplied on a scale of equal amplitude. The establishment also possessed some fine pictures, original and from the first masters. The removal of these was impossible, and hence the reluctance of the Mother Superior to leave her house was sufficiently natural. Assured, besides, of safety, she remained until further delay would have perilled the safety of her innocent and numerous flock. This lady marshalled her procession with great good sense, coolness and decision. They were instructed to secure the clothes most suitable to their protection from the weather, and to take with them those valuables which were portable; and, accompanied by Rev. Dr. O'Connell and others, the damsels filed on, under the lead of their Superior, through long tracts of fire, burning roofs, tumbling walls, wading through billows of flame, and taking, at first, the pathway to St. Peter's (Catholic) Church. Blinding fires left them almost aimless in their march; but they succeeded in reaching the desired point in safety. Here, on strips of bedding, quilts and coverlets, the young girls found repose, protected by the vigilance of a few gentlemen, their priest, and, we believe, by two officers of the Yankee army, whose names are given as Colonel Corley and Dr. Galaghan. To these gentlemen, both Catholic Irish, the Mother Superior acknowledges her great indebtedness.

They had need of all the watch and vigilance of these persons. It was soon found that several soldiers followed them in their flight, and were making attempts to fire the edifice on several sides. These attempts, repeatedly baffled and as often renewed, showed at length so tenacious a purpose for its destruction, that it was thought best to leave the building and seek refuge in the church-yard, and there, in the cold and chill, and among the grave-stones with the dead, these terrified living ones remained, trembling watchers through the rest of this dreary night.

The Presbyterian grave-yard had a number of families quartered in it for several days after the destruction of the city. Aged ladies and young children were also exposed in open lots until after the Federals left the city.

We here borrow freely from a communication made by the Rev. Lawrence P. O'Connell to the Catholic *Pacificator*. He so fully reports the fate of St. Mary's College, that nothing need be added to it. We have simply abridged such portions of his statement as might be dispensed with in this connection:

"St. Mary's College, founded in 1852, by the Rev. J. J. O'Connell, Pastor of the Catholics in Columbia, was robbed, pillaged and then given to the flames. The College was a very fine brick building, and capable of accommodating over one hundred students. It had an excellent library attached, which was selected with great care, and with no limited view to expense. It also possessed several magnificent paintings, executed in Rome, and presented to the institution by kind patrons. Besides the property belonging to St. Mary's College, that of four priests, who were its professors and lived there, was also consumed. Each, as is always the case amongst the Catholic clergy, had his individual collection of books, paintings, statuary, sacred pictures, &c. Nobody who is not a rigorous student and a lover of literature can possibly realize the losses sustained by these gentlemen. Manuscripts of rare value, notes taken from lectures of the most eminent men in Europe and America, orations, sermons, &c., are treasures not often valued by the vulgar, but to the compiler they are more priceless than diamonds. Of those who lost all in St. Mary's, three are brothers, viz: Revs. Jeremiah J. O'Connell, Lawrence P. O'Connell, Joseph P. O'Connell, D. D.; and the other, Rev. Augustus J. McNeal."

The Post Chaplain, the author of the report from which we draw, was the only clergyman in the College when it was destroyed. He was made a prisoner, and, though pleading to be allowed to save the holy oils, &c., his prayer was rejected. A sacrilegious squad drank their whiskey from the sacred chalice. The sacred vestments and consecrated vessels used for the celebration of the mass—all things, indeed, pertaining to the exercise of sacerdotal functions—were profaned and stolen. Of the College itself, and the property which it contained, nothing was saved but the massed ruins, which show where the fabric stood. The clergymen saved nothing beyond the garments which they had upon their persons.

CHAPTER XVIII.

THE SOUTH CAROLINA COLLEGE—VALUABLE PRIVATE LIBRARIES, ETC.

The destruction of private libraries and valuable collections of objects of art and *virtu,* was very large in Columbia. It was by the urgent entreaties of the Rev. Mr. Porter, the professors and others, that the safety of the South Carolina College library was assured. The buildings were occupied by Confederate hospitals, where some three hundred invalids and convalescents found harborage.

In a conversation with the Rev. Mr. Porter, regarding the safety of the College Library, General Sherman indulged in a sneer. "I would rather," said he, "give you books than destroy them. I am sure your people need them very much."[7] To this

---

[7] Sherman was but echoing the falsehood which he had heard all his life from the inherent haters of South Carolina: that its people were not educated or not readers. What were such people doing with a handsome library—constructed exclusively for and used exclusively as a library—containing one of the finest collections of books in the United States, including an unusual collection of incunabula—if they did not read? Perhaps Sherman wanted them to confine their reading to those political primers that

Mr. Porter made no reply, suffering the General to rave for awhile upon a favorite text with him, the glories of his flag and the perpetuation of the Union, which he solemnly pledged himself to maintain against all the fates.

That his own people did not value books, in any proper degree, may be shown by their invariable treatment of libraries. These were almost universally destroyed, tumbled into the weather, the streets, gutters, hacked and hewn and trampled, even when the collections were of the rarest value and immense numbers. Libraries of ten thousand volumes—books such as cannot again be procured—were sacrificed. It will suffice to illustrate the numerous losses of this sort in Columbia, to report the fate of the fine collections of Dr. R. W. Gibbes. This gentleman, a man of letters and science, a *virtuoso*, busied all his life in the accumulation of works of arts and literature, and rare objects of intense interest to the amateur and student, has been long known to the American world, North and South, in the character of a *savant*. Perhaps no other person in South Carolina has more distinguished himself by his scientific writings, and by the indefatigable research which illustrated them, by the accumulation of proofs from the natural world. A friendly correspondent gives us a mournful narrative of the disasters to his house, his home, his manuscripts and his various and valuable collections, from which we condense the following particulars:

"Besides the fine mansion of Dr. Gibbes, and its usual contents of furniture, his real estate on Main street, &c., his scientific collections and paintings were of immense value, occasioning more regret than could arise from any loss of mere property. His gallery contained upwards of *two hundred paintings*, among which were pictures by Washington Allston, Sully, Inman, Charles Fraser and DeVeaux; and many originals and copies by European hands, were highly prized from their intrinsic ex-

---

taught that a sovereign state that had voluntarily entered a union with other states had no right to voluntarily withdraw from that union, and that in case it did withdraw a part of the other states to the agreement had a legal right to conquer that state and force it back into the union and that the legality of that action was to be determined by the executive and not the judicial branch of the general government. There would have been many hundreds of thousands more books in South Carolina at the moment that Sherman spoke if there had been any sincerity behind his observation. Simms's magnificent library at Woodlands and General D. F. Jamison's at Burwood nearby were both destroyed, as was the State Library of South Carolina containing twenty-five thousand volumes.

cellence and interesting associations. The family portraits in the collection were also numerous—some ancient, all valuable; and several admirable busts graced his drawing-room. His portfolios contained collections of the best engravings, from the most famous pictures of the old masters and by the most excellent engravers of the age. These were mostly a bequest from the venerable C. Fraser, who was one of those who best knew what a good engraving or picture should be, and who had, all his life, been engaged in accumulating the most valuable illustrations of the progress of art.[8] Nor was the library of Dr. Gibbes less rich in stores of letters and science, art and medicine. His historical collection was particularly rich, especially in American and South Carolina history. His cabinet of Southern fossils and memorials, along with those brought from the remotest regions, was equally select and extensive. It contained no less than ten thousand specimens. The collection of shark's teeth was pronounced by Agassiz to be the finest in the world. His collections of historical documents, original correspondence of the Revolution, especially that of South Carolina, was exceedingly large and valuable. From these he had compiled and edited three volumes, and had there arrested the publication, in order to transfer his *material* to the South Carolina Historical Society. All are now lost.[9] So, also, was his collection of autographs—the letters of eminent correspondents in every department of letters, science and art. Many relics of our aborigines, others from the pyramids and tombs of Egypt, of Herculaneum, Pompeii and Mexico, with numerous memorials from the Revolutionary and recent battle-fields of our country, shared the same

---

[8] A bust of Dr. Gibbes by Hiram Powers. whom he had helped, and one of the Doctor's little son DeVeaux, by Henry Kirke Brown, were saved, and are now owned by his grandson, Dr. R. W. Gibbes, of Columbia. Brown worked in Columbia from 1857 to 1861 on a large pediment for the State House. That also was destroyed by Sherman's men. (See *Art and Artists of the Capitol of the United States of America*, 193.) The Powers bust was thrown over Dr. Gibbes's back fence into an adjoining yard where it was found later. The Brown bust had been sent to a sister in an Up-Country town a few days before Sherman arrived.

[9] Simms was mistaken as to this. The General Assembly of South Carolina had partially financed the publication of these volumes and Dr. Gibbes had presented to the State many of the papers that had been printed therein. They were saved with other State records when the Secretary of State (Col. Wm. R. Huntt) and Professor William J. Rivers shipped them off to the Up-Country before Sherman's army arrived. They are now in the custody of the Historical Commission of South Carolina in the World War Memorial, at Columbia.

fate—are gone down to the same abyss of ruin. The records of the Surgeon-General's Department of the State, from its organization, no longer exist. The dwelling which contained these inestimable treasures was deliberately fired by men, for whose excuse no whiskey influence could be .pleaded. They were quite as sober as in a thousand other cases where they sped with the torch of the incendiary. It was fired in the owner's presence, and when he expostulated with them, he was laughed to scorn. A friend who sought to extinguish the fire kindled in his very parlor, was seized by the collar and hurled aside, with the ejaculation, "Let the d—d house burn."

CHAPTER XIX.

PROFFERED ASSISTANCE—THE LADY'S PLUME AND RIDING WHIP.

It was one almost invariable feature of the numerous melancholy processions of fugitive women and children and old men escaping from their burning houses, to be escorted by Federal officers or soldiers—as frequently by the one as by the other—who sometimes pretended civility, and mixed it up with jeering or offensive remarks upon their situation. These civilities had an ulterior object. To accept them, under the notion that they were tendered in good faith, was to be robbed or insulted. The young girl carrying work-box or bundle, who could be persuaded to trust it to the charge of one of the men, very often lost possession of it wholly.

"That trunk is small, but it seems heavy," quoth one to a young lady, who, in the procession of the nuns, was carrying off her mother's silver.

"What's in it, I wonder? Let me carry it."

"No thank you. My object is to save it, if I can."

"Well, I'll save it for you; let me help you."

"No; I need no help of yours, and wish you to understand that I mean to save it, if I can."

"You are too proud, miss! but we'll humble you yet. You have been living in clover all your life—we'll bring you down to the wash-tub. Those white hands shall be done brown in the sun before we're done with you.[10]

Officers, even ranking as high as colonels, were found as active in the work of insults and plunder as any of their common men. One of these colonels came into the presence of a young girl, a pupil at the Convent, and the daughter of a distinguished public man. He wore in his hat her riding plume, attached by a small golden ornament, and in his hands he carried her riding whip. She calmly addressed him thus:

"I have been robbed, sir, of every article of clothing and ornaments; even the dress I wear is borrowed. I am resigned to their loss. But there are some things that I would not willingly lose. You have in your cap the plume from my riding hat—you carry in your hand my riding whip. They were gifts to me from a precious friend. I demand them from you."

"Oh! these cannot be yours—I have had them a long time."

"You never had them before last night. It was then I lost them. They are mine, and the gold ornament of the feather engraved with the initials of the giver. Once more I demand them of you."

"Well, I'm willing to *give* them to you, if you'll accept them as a keepsake."

"No, sir; I wish no keep-sake of your's; I shall have sufficiently painful memories to remind me of those whom I could never willingly see again—whom I have never wished to see."

"Oh! I rather guess you're right there," with a grin.

"Will you restore me my whip and feather?"

"As a keep-sake! Yes."

"No, sir; as my property—which you can only wear as stolen property."

"I tell you, if you'll take them as a keep-sake from me, you shall have them."

---

[10] The prosperity of the planter population of the South long aroused the envy and the enmity of many people of the Eastern States who preached that it was built upon the toil of slaves, but they said nothing of their own sweat shops and poorly paid factory hands. It was before the days of labor unions, and the masses were not yet seeing for themselves.

"You must then keep them, sir—happy, perhaps, that you *cannot* blush whenever you sport the plume or flourish the whip." And he bore off the treasures of the damsel.

In these connections, oaths of the most blasphemous kind were rarely foreborne, even when their talk was had with females. The troops had a large faith in Sherman's generalship. One of their lieutenants is reported to have said: "He's all hell at flanking. He'd flank God Almighty out of Heaven and the devil into hell."

CHAPTER XX.

THE CATHEDRAL—"THE WAR UPON WOMEN"—CURIOUS HOUSE-BUILDING—THE STAYS IN THE WRONG PLACE.

But this is enough on this topic, and we must plead the exactions of truth and the necessities of historical evidence, to justify us in repeating and recording such monstrous blasphemies. We shall hereafter, from other hands, be able to report some additional dialogues held with the women of Columbia, by some of the Federal officers. Of their *temper,* one or two more brief anecdotes will suffice.

The Convent, among its other possessions, had a very beautiful model of the Cathedral, of Charleston. This occupied a place in the Convent ground. It was believed to have been destroyed by the soldiers. One of the nuns lamented its fate to the Mother Superior, in the presence of Colonel Ewell, (?) an aid of one of the generals. He muttered bitterly, "Yes; it is rightly served; and I could wish the same fate to befall every cathedral in which *Te Deum* has been performed at the downfall of our glorious flag."

A gentleman was expressing to one of the Federal generals the fate of the Convent, and speaking of the losses, especially of the Lady Superior, he replied dryly: "It is not forgotten that this lady is the sister of Bishop Lynch, who had *Te Deum* performed in his cathedral at the fall of Fort Sumter."

A lady of this city spoke indignantly to General Atkins, of Sherman's army, and said of that general, "He wars upon women."

"Yes," said Atkins, "and justly. It is the women of the South who keep up this cursed rebellion. It gave us the greatest satisfaction to see those proud Georgia women begging crumbs from Yankee leavings; and this will soon be the fate of all you Carolina women."

Escorting a sad procession of fugitives from the burning dwellings, one of the soldiers said:

"What a glorious sight!"

"Terribly so," said one of the ladies.

"Grand!" said he.

"Very pitiful," was the reply.

The lady added:

"How, as men, you can behold the horrors of this scene, and behold the sufferings of these innocents, without terrible pangs of self-condemnation and self-loathing, it is difficult to conceive."

"We glory in it!" was the answer. "I tell you, madam, that when the people of the North hear of the vengeance we have meted out to your city, there will be one universal shout of rejoicing from man, woman and child, from Maine to Maryland."[11]

"You are, then, sir, only a fitting representative of your people."

Another, who had forced himself as an escort upon a party, on the morning of Saturday, said, pointing to the thousand stacks of chimneys, "You are a curious people here in housebuilding. You run up your chimneys before you build the house."

One who had been similarly impudent, said to a mother, who was bearing a child in her arms:

"Let me carry the baby, madam."

---

[11] That was the feeling of millions of ignorant people of the North who were taught from infancy by politicians of their section to hate the South. The said politicians' sole purpose was to wreck the prosperity of the South and destroy its political leadership. They accomplished the first, but whenever there is a Democratic administration in Washington, whether in Congress or the executive or both, that Southern leadership persists, even 'though the Northern congressmen of the party far outnumber the Southern congressmen.

"Do not touch him for your life," was the reply. "I would sooner hurl him into the flames and plunge in after him than that he should be polluted by your touch. Nor shall a child of mine ever have even the show of obligation to a Yankee!"

"Well, that's going it strong, by——; but I like your pluck. We like it d—e; and you'll see us coming back after the war—every man of us—to get a Carolina wife. We hate your men like h—l, but we love your women!"

"We much prefer your hate, even though it comes in fire. Will you leave us, sir?"

It was not always, however, that our women were able to preserve their coolness and firmness under the assaults. We have quite an amusing story of a luckless wife, who was confronted by a stalwart soldier, with a horrid oath and a cocked revolver at her head.

"Your watch! your money! you d—d rebel b—h!"

The horrid oaths, the sudden demand, fierce look and rapid action, so terrified her that she cried out, "Oh! my G—d! I have no watch, no money, except what's tied round my waist!"

We need not say how deftly the Bowie-knife was applied to loose the stays of the lady.

She was then taught, for the first time in her life, that the stays were wrongly placed. They should have been upon her tongue.

In all their conversation, the officers exhibited a very bombastic manner, and their exaggerations of their strength and performances great and frequent. On their first arrival they claimed generally to have sixty thousand men; in a few hours after, the number was swollen to seventy-five thousand; by night, it had reached one hundred thousand; and on Saturday, the day after, they claimed to have one hundred and twenty-five thousand. We have already estimated the real number at forty thousand—total cavalry, infantry and artillery.[12]

---

[12] His estimate was fifty thousand, on page 5.

CHAPTER XXI.

THE SOUTH CAROLINA COLLEGE—DANGER FROM FALLING
SPARKS—EXCITEMENT AMONG THE INMATES—DRUNKEN
CAVALRY—A FEDERAL OFFICER DOING HIS DUTY—THE
LEGISLATIVE LIBRARY.

We have already passingly adverted to the difficulty of saving the South Carolina College library from the flames, and lest
we should have conveyed a false impression in respect to the
degree of effort made in saving it, we give some particulars
which may be found of interest. We need scarcely say that the
professors clung to their sacred charge with a tenacity which
never once abandoned it or forebore the exertions necessary for
its safety; while the officers of the several hospitals, to which
the College buildings were generally given up, were equally
prompt to give their co-operation. Very soon after the entrance
of the Federals into the city, Dr. Thompson, of the hospital,
with Professors LaBorde, Reynolds and Rivers, took their places
at the gate of the College Campus, and awaited their approach.
Towards noon, a body of soldiers, led by a Captain Young, made
their appearance at the gate, and the surgeon, with the professors, made a special appeal to the captain for the protection of
the library and the College buildings; to which he replied with a
solemn assurance that the place should be spared, and that he
would station a sufficient guard within and without the walls.
He remarked, with some surprise, upon the great size of the
enclosure and establishment. The guard was placed, and no
serious occasion for alarm was experienced throughout the day;
but, from an early hour of the night, the buildings began to be
endangered by showers of sparks from contiguous houses, which
fell upon their roofs. This danger increased hour by hour, as
the flames continued to advance, and finally, the roofs of the
several dwellings of Professors LaBorde and Rivers burst out
in flames. Their families were forced to fly, and it required all
the efforts of professors, surgeons, servants, even aided by a
file of soldiers, to arrest the conflagration. Every building within the campus was thus in danger. The destruction of any one
building would to a certainty have led to the loss of all. The
most painful apprehensions were quickened into a sense of horror, when the feeble inmates of the hospital were remembered.
There were numbers of noble soldiers, brave Kentuckians and

others, desperately wounded, to whom—lacking, as the establishment did at that moment, the necessary labor—but little assistance could be rendered. They were required to shift for themselves, while the few able-bodied men within the campus were on the housetops fighting the fire. The poor fellows were to be seen dragging their maimed and feeble bodies, as best they could, along the floors, adown the stairs, and crawling out, with great pain and labor, and by the tardiest process, into that atmosphere of reeking flame, which now girdled the establishment. Others, again, unable to leave their beds, resigned themselves to their fate. We can better conceive than describe the terrible agonies, to them, of those hours of dreadful anticipation in which they lay. Happily, the fires were subdued by 4 in the morning of Saturday.

But the danger, even then, was not over. About 8 A. M., the College gate was assaulted by a band of drunken cavalry, one hundred and fifty or more, bent upon penetrating the campus, and swearing to fire the buildings. The officer in command of the guard reported to the professors that his force was not adequate to the protection of the establishment, and that he was about to be overwhelmed.

Professors LaBorde and Rivers, followed by Surgeon Thompson, at once sped, in all haste, to the headquarters of General Howard, appealing to him, in the most passionate terms, to redeem his pledge for the protection of the College and its library. He promptly commanded his Chief of Staff, Colonel Stone, to repair to the scene and arrest the danger. This—revolver in hand—he promptly did, and succeeded in dispersing the incendiary cavalry.

It is with profound regret that we add that the Legislative library, consisting of twenty-five thousand choice volumes, was wholly destroyed in the old Capitol.

––––––––

CHAPTER XXII.

THE MASONS AND ODD FELLOWS—FRATERNIZATION—THE CROMWELL SWORD.

Among the moral and charitable institutions which suffered greatly in the fire, were the several Masonic bodies. They lost everything, with rare exceptions; houses, lodges, regalias, charts, charters, jewels, and every form of implement and paraphernalia. Much of this property had been accumulated in Columbia from Charleston and other places—had been sent hither for safe keeping. Their losses will for a long while be wholly irreparable, and cannot be repaired, unless, indeed, through the liberality of remote and wealthy fraternities in other sections. The furniture and jewels were, in the largest number of cases, of the richest and most valuable order, wholly of silver, and in great proportion were gifts and bequests of favorite brothers who had reached the highest ranks in the order. We enumerate the following lodges as the chief sufferers:

1. Richland Lodge No. 39, A. F. M.
2. Acacia Lodge No. 94, A. F. M.
3. True Brotherhood Lodge No. 84, A. F. M.
[These all met in Columbia.]
4. Union Kilwinning No. 4, A. F. M.
5. Orange No. 14, A. F. M.
[These met in Charleston.]
6. Carolina Chapter No. 1, R. A. M.
7. Columbia Chapter No. 5, R. A. M.
8. Union Council No. 5, R. A. M.
9. Enoch Lodge of Perfection—Ineffable Degrees.
10. DeMolay Council, Knights of Kadosch—Ineffable Degrees.

The Independent Order of Odd Fellows and other orders were sufferers in like degree with the Masonic bodies. These were:

1. Palmetto Lodge No. 5.
2. Congaree Lodge No. 29.
3. Eutaw Encampment Lodge No. 2.
4. Sons of Temperance.
5. Sons of Malta.

The buildings, chambers, and lodges which contained the treasures of these bodies, were first plundered and then given to the flames. The soldiers were to be seen about the streets, dressed up in the aprons, scarfs and regalias. Some of the Federal Masons were active in endeavoring to arrest the robbers in their work, but without success. In a conversation with one of the Western Masons, he responded to the signs and behaved courteously, but he said: "We are told that all fraternization with your Masonic bodies of the South has been cut off, in consequence of your Masons renouncing all connection or tie between them and the Masons of the North." We replied to him that the story was absurd, and evidently set afloat in order to prevent the *Northern* Masons from affording succor to a Southern brother in the hour of his distress—that Masonry overrides the boundaries of States, allows of no political or religious differences, and that its very nature and constitution are adverse to the idea of any such renunciations of the paramount duties of the craft, in all countries and under all circumstances.

We add a few particulars in relation to some of these lodges, showing the extent and character of their losses. The minutes of Union Kilwinning Lodge No. 4, were more than a century old; those of Orange Lodge No. 14, very near a century. These are all gone, and the loss is irremediable. A portion of the minutes of Richland Lodge No. 39 are supposed to be safe, as they were confided to the keeping of a Masonic writer, with a view to the preparation of a history.

Among the items of loss, which are particularly lamented, that of the famous sword of State, called "the Cromwell Sword," belonging to the Grand Lodge of South Carolina, is particularly deplored. This was an antique of peculiar interest and value. Its history, as given by Dalcho, may be given here, as particularly calculated to gratify the curious, as well as the Masonic reader. It was a large, elegant and curious two-edged weapon, in a rich velvet scabbard, highly ornamented with Masonic emblems, and with the arms of the Grand Master. It had been presented to the Grand Lodge by the Provincial Grand Master, after the installation of the grand officers, was given as a consecrated sword, and received with reverent assurances, to keep it safely, so far as human effort could accord safety. The weapon had been long in the possession of the Grand Master's family, and was said to have once belonged to Oliver Cromwell, a legend to which some degree of probability may be given, from the fact that the Provincial Grand Master was a descendant of Sir Edward Leigh, who was a member of the Long Parliament and a Parliamentary General in the time of the Protector, from whom, perhaps, he received it.

The farther history of this sword may as well be given here. From the time of the presentation it continued in the possession of the Grand Lodge, and was borne by the Grand Sword Bearer, or in later times, the Grand Pursuivant, in all public processions. At length, at the conflagration which, in the year 1838, destroyed so large a portion of the city of Charleston, and with other buildings the Masonic Hall, the sword was, with great difficulty, saved by brother Samuel Seyle, the Grand Tiler, with the loss of the hilt, the scabbard, and a small part of the extremity of the blade. In the confusion consequent on the fire, the sword thus mutilated was mislaid, and for a long time it was supposed to be lost. In 1852, a committee was appointed by the Grand Lodge to make every exertion for its recovery, and, at length, in the beginning of the year 1854, it was accidentally found by the Grand Tiler, in an out-house on his premises, and was by him restored to the Grand Lodge in its mutilated condition. The lost piece of the blade was ingenously replaced by a cutler in the city of Charleston, and being sent to New York, was returned with new hilt and velvet scabbard, and was used in its appropriate place during the centennial ceremonies of that year.

With such a history, and blended with such tradition of its origin, we need not feel surprised at the universal and keen feeling occasioned by its loss.

CHAPTER XXIII.

ANOTHER DAY OF HORRORS—WHEN WILL IT END?—THE BUGLES—BLACKENED WALLS—SYMPATHIZING SOLDIERS.

The morning of Saturday, the 18th of February, opened still with its horrors and terrors, though somewhat diminished in their intensity. A lady said to an officer at her house, somewhere about 4 o'clock that morning:

"In the name of God, sir, when is this work of hell to be ended?"

He replied: "You will hear the bugles at sunrise, when a guard will enter the town and withdraw these troops. It will then cease, and not before."

Sure enough, with the bugle's sound, and the entrance of fresh bodies of troops, there was an instantaneous arrest of incendiarism. You could see the rioters carried off in groups and squads, from the several precincts they had ravaged, and those which they still meditated to destroy.

The tap of the drum, the sound of the signal cannon, could not have been more decisive in its effect, more prompt and complete. But two fires were *set*, among private dwellings, after sunrise; and the flames only went up from a few places, where the fire had been last applied; and these were rapidly expiring.

The best and most beautiful portion of Columbia lay in ruins. Never was ruin more complete; and the sun rose with a wan countenance, peering dimly through the dense vapors which seemed wholly to overspread the firmament. Very miserable was the spectacle. On every side ruins, and smoking masses of blackened walls, and towers of grim, ghastly chimneys, and between, in desolate groups, reclining on mattress, or bed, or earth, were wretched women and children, gazing vacantly on the site of a once blessed abode of home and innocence.

Roving detachments of the soldiers passed around and among them. There were those who looked and lingered nigh, with taunt and sarcasm. Others there were, in whom humanity did not seem wholly extinguished; and others again, to their credit, be it said, who were truly sorrowful and sympathizing, who had labored for the safety of family and property, and who openly deplored the dreadful crime, which threatened the lives and honors of the one, and destroyed so completely the other.

CHAPTER XXIV

THE DESTRUCTION OF PUBLIC BUILDINGS—EXPLOSION OF SHELLS—LOSS OF LIFE—THE STATE CAPITOL—HEAVY LOSS TO THE STATE.

But we have no time for description. The relentless fate was hurrying forward, and the destroyer had still as large a share of his assigned labors to execute. This day was devoted to the destruction of those buildings of a public character which had escaped the wreck of the city proper.

The Saluda cotton manufactory, the property of Colonel L. D. Childs, was burned by the troops prior to their entry of the city and on their approach to it, the previous day. The several powder mills were destroyed on Saturday. The Arsenal buildings (State and Confederate) on Sunday, and it is understood that in the attempt to haul away ammunition from the latter place, the Federals lost a large number of men, from an unlooked for explosion. It is reported in one case that no less than forty men, with their officers—the entire company—were blown to pieces in one precinct, and half as many in another. But the facts can never be precisely ascertained. The body of a Federal captain lay on the banks of the river for several days.

The magnificant steam printing establishment of Evans & Cogswell—with the house assigned to their engravers, and another house, stored with stationery and book stock—perhaps the most complete establishment of the kind in the Southern States —was destroyed on Saturday. These were all private property, most of it isolated in situation, and deliberately fired.

So, the fearful progress of incendiarism continued throughout Saturday and Sunday, nor did it wholly cease on Monday. The gas works—one of the great necessities of the people—was then deliberately destroyed; and it was with some difficulty that the water works were saved.

The cotton card manufactory of the State; the sword factory —a private interest; the stocking manufactory—private; the buildings at Fair Grounds, adjoining cemetery; the several railway depots; Alexander's foundry; the South Carolina Railroad foundry and work shops; the Government armory, and other buildings of greater or less value, partly Government and partly private property—all shared a common fate.

Major Niernsee, the State Architect, was a great loser, in his implements and valuable scientific and professional library.

The new Capitol building, being unfinished, and not likely to be finished in many years—useless, accordingly to us—was spared—only suffering from some petty assaults of malice. Here and there, a plinth fractured; here and there a Corinthian capital. The beautiful pillar of Tennessee marble was thus injured. So, at great pains-taking, the soldiers calmbered up on ladders to reach and efface the exquisite scroll and ornamental work on the face of the building—disfiguring the beautiful chiseling which had wrought out the vine and acorn tracery on the several panels; and the bundles of *fasces,* on the Northern part, were fractured or broken away in parts.

The statue of Washington, in bronze, cast in 1858, for the city of Charleston,[13] from Houdon's original, in the rotunda at Richmond, received several bruises from brickbats, addressed to face and breast. A shell scratched his back, and the staff which he bore in his hand was broken off in the middle. But the bronze seems to have defied destruction and may be considered still perfect.

The bust of Calhoun, by Powers, was totally destroyed; so, also, was the ideal personification, by the sculptor Brown, of the Genius of Liberty.[14]

A large collection of complete capitals, destined for the Capitol, and lying in the open square, were destroyed either by the heat of the contiguous fire, or by explosions of gun-powder introduced among them. Hereafter, such beautiful pieces of workmanship might be kept more safely and certainly, by being buried deeply in excavations of sand.

The iron Palmetto tree, that ingenious performance of Werner, of Charleston, dedicated as a monument to the Palmetto Regiment, so renowned in the war with Mexico, suffered the loss of a number of its lower and larger branches; but these, we think, may be restored at comparatively little cost. The apartment in the base was torn open, having been wrenched from its fastenings, but no other mischief seems to have been done to it. It was probably spared, as commemorating the deeds of those who had fought under their own flag.

An officer connected with the State Capitol, furnishes the following particulars:

The new State Capitol presented a very conspicuous mark to the cannon on Lexington heights, yet fortunately sustained but little injury—none, indeed, which cannot be easily repaired. Five

---

13 This is an error. The W. J. Hubard Foundry, of Richmond, had cast six bronze copies of Houdon's marble statue of Washington which stands in the Capitol in Richmond and offered them for sale at ten thousand dollars apiece. One was bought for South Carolina by Governor R. F. W. Allston in 1858 and paid for by legislative appropriations.

14 See note 8, page 64. There was also lost with the State Library a bust of Andrew Jackson, which had been presented to "his native State" by James Thonaldson, of Philadelphia.

shots struck the West end, yet none of them did any serious damage, except one. This shattered the ornamented sill and ballusters of one of the corridors of the principal floor. Another shell injured a fluted column on the centre projection. Two shots hit the interior of the brick arch over the Eastern front centre window, and two other shots struck and slightly scaled off the granite jamb division of the treble centre window in the Eastern front.

When in possession, the soldiers tried to deface and defile as much as they could. They wrote their names in pencil on the marble, giving their companies and regiments, and sometimes coupling appropriately foul comments with their signatures, thus addressed to posterity. They seem to have found considerable sport in their practice, with brick-bats, or fragments of rocks, as sharp-shooters; and making the fine bronze statue of Washington their mark, they won various successes against his face, breast and legs. Sundry bruises and abrasions are to be found upon the head and front, and a part of his cane has been carried away among their *spolia opima.*[15] The finely sculptured oak leaf decorations of the marble door pilasters at the main entrance door of the principal floor over the Northern front, as well as the ornaments of the soffit of that door, have been seriously defaced. The beaks of the eagles, in the panels above, and to the right and left of that doorway, as also the lower portions of the *fasces* on each side of the same, have been beaten out. The corner, or groin stones, and basement cornice at the South-western corner of the building, were also damaged to some extent by the fire from the adjacent old State House building.

But all the injuries to the structure were insignificant in comparison with that which was done to the finished and raw material within the precinct—the wrought and rude marble, granite, iron and machinery; the work completed in these materials, and which has been accumulating for the last four years in yard and work-shop—in all this, our loss has been very great. There were destroyed among those accumulations forty beautifully

---

[15] On the Missouri red granite base (supplied about 1909) upon which the statue stands, the writer, with an appropriation by the General Assembly, has placed a bronze tablet testifying to the facts here stated. The cane has not been repaired, as broken it preserves history and at the same time is an object lesson of what the passions of war will do; destroy respect for the national heroes of those who are doing the destroying.

sculptured Corinthian capitals, designed for the two large porticoes of the edifice, and wrought in our own beautiful native granite; the Corinthian capitals wrought in Italian marble for the great marble hall and stair-cases on the principal floor in the interior; all the polished shafts, in Tennessee marble, for the latter; and nearly all the marble work and pavements for the whole building, in Tennessee and Italian marble—together with the granite ballustrade and railings surmounting the main building and for the surrounding terrace.   To these, add the destruction of hundreds of immense unwrought blocks of granite and marble of every description—machinery, tools; the sculptor's atelier and work-shops, containing all the models and some of the unfinished statues meant for the main gable field or tympanum of the Northern front; the original models of the medallion portraits of Hayne and McDuffie, and one of the latest and best casts of the head of Calhoun.   But one small store house remains uninjured 'throughout the premises, containing some finished marble work, the monolith granite columns of the main porticoes, and some completed work for the main cornice of the structure.   The total pecuniary loss to the State, in the damage thus done to the new capitol, and to the material designed for it, including tools, instruments, models, &c., can fall very little short of one million of dollars in specie.

CHAPTER XXV.

TREATMENT OF THE NEGROES—GENERAL SHERMAN AND THE DEAD NEGRO—WHO CAUSED THE WAR.

Something should be said in respect to the manner in which the negroes were treated by the Federals while in Columbia, and as regards the influences employed by which to beguile or take them from their owners.   We have already adverted to the fact that there was a vast difference between the feelings and performances of the men from the West, and those coming, or directly emanating, from the Eastern States.   The former were adverse to a connection with them; but few negroes were to be seen among these, and they were simply used as drudges, grooming horses, bearing burdens, humble of demeanor and rewarded with kicks, cuffs and curses, frequently without provocation. They despised and disliked the negro; openly professed their scorn or hatred, declared their unwillingness to have them as companions in arms or in company at all.

Several instances have been given us of their modes of repelling the association of the negro, usually with blow of the fist, butt of the musket, slash of the sword or prick of the bayonet.

Sherman himself looked on these things indifferently, if we are to reason from a single fact afforded us by Mayor Goodwyn. This gentleman, while walking with the general, heard the report of a gun. Both heard it, and immediately proceeded to the spot. There they found a group of soldiers, with a stalwart young negro fellow lying dead before them on the street, the body yet warm and bleeding. Pushing it with his feet, Sherman said, in his quick, hasty manner:

"What does this mean, boys?"

The reply was sufficiently cool and careless. "The d—d black rascal gave us his impudence, and we shot him."

"Well, bury him at once! Get him out of sight!"

As they passed on, one of the party remarked:

"Is that the way, General, you treat such a case?"

"Oh!" said he, "we have no time now for courts martial and things of that sort!"

A lady showed us a coverlet, with huge holes burned in it, which she said had covered a sleeping negro woman, when the Yankees threw their torches into her bed, from which she was narrowly extricated with life.

Of the recklessness of these soldiers, especially when sharpened by cupidity, an instance is given where they thrust their bayonets into a bed, where they fancied money to be hidden, between two sleeping children—being, it is admitted, somewhat careful not to strike through the bodies of the children.

The treatment of the negroes in their houses was, in the larger proportion of cases, quite as harsh as that which was shown to the whites. They were robbed in like manner, frequently stripped of every article of clothing and provisions, and where the wigwam was not destroyed, it was effectually gutted. Few negroes having a good hat, good pair of shoes, good overcoat, but were incontinently deprived of them, and roughly handled when they remonstrated. These acts, we believe, were mostly ascribed to Western men. They were repeatedly heard to say: "We are Western men, and don't want your d——d black faces among us."

When addressing the negro, they frequently charged him with being the cause of the war. In speaking to the whites on this subject, especially to South Carolinians, the cause was ascribed to them. In more than one instance, we were told:

"We are going to burn this d——d town. We've begun and we'll go through. *This thing began here*, and we'll stack the houses and burn the town."

A different *role* was assigned to, or self-assumed by, the Eastern men. They hob-a-nobbed with the negro, walked with him, and smoked and joked with him. Filled his ears with all sorts of blarney; lured him, not only with hopes of freedom, but all manner of license. They hovered about the premises of the citizens, seeking all occasion to converse with the negroes. They would elude the guards, slip into the kitchens, if the gates were open, or climb over the rear fence and converse with all who would listen. No doubt they succeeded in beguiling many, since nothing is more easy than to seduce, with promises of prosperity, ease and influence, the laboring classes of any people, white or black. To teach them that they are badly governed and suffering wrong, is the favorite method of demagogueism in all countries, and is that sort of influence which will always prevail with a people at once vain, sensual and ignorant. But, as far as we have been able to see and learn, a large proportion of the negroes were carried away forcibly. When the beguiler failed to seduce, he resorted to violence.

The soldiers, in several cases which have been reported to us, pursued the slaves with the tenacity of blood-hounds; were at their elbows when they went forth, and hunted them up, at all hours, on the premises of the owner. Very frequent are instances where the negro, thus hotly pursued, besought protection of his master or mistress, sometimes voluntarily seeking a hiding place along the swamps of the river; at other times, finding it under the bed of the owner; and not leaving these places of refuge till long after the troops had departed.

For fully a month after they had gone, the negroes, singly or in squads, were daily making their way back to Columbia, having escaped from the Federals by dint of great perseverance and cunning, generally in wretched plight, half-starved and with little clothing. They represented the difficulties in the way of their escape to be very great, the officers placing them finally under guards at night, and that they could only succeed in flight at the peril of life or limb. Many of these were negroes of Columbia, but the larger proportion seemed to hail from Barnwell. They all sought passports to return to their owners and plantations.

CHAPTER XXVI.

THE ADJACENT COUNTRY—HORSES, MULES, ETC., CARRIED OFF OR KILLED—VEHICLES DESTROYED—RAPE—TORTURE.

We should not overlook the ravage and destruction in the immediate precincts of the city, though beyond its corporate boundaries. Within a few miles of Columbia, from two to five miles, it was girdled by beautiful country seats, such as those of the Hampton family—Millwood—a place famous of yore for its charm and elegance of society, its frank hospitality and the lavish bounty of its successive hosts. The destruction of this family seat of opulence, and grace, and hospitality, will occasion sensation in European countries, no less than in our own, among those who have enjoyed its grateful privileges, as guests, in better days.

The beautiful country seats of Mr. Secretary Trenholm, of Dr. John Wallace, Mrs. Thomas Stark, Colonel Thomas Taylor, Captain James U. Adams, Mr. C. P. Pelham, (Mill Creek,) as well as homestead—and many more—all shared the fate of Millwood—all were robbed and ruined, then given to the flames; and from these places were carried off all horses, mules, cattle, hogs and stock of every sort; and the provisions not carried off, were destroyed.

In many cases, where mules and horses were not choice, they were shot down. But this was the common history. On all the farms and plantations, and along the road sides everywhere, for many a mile, horses, mules and cattle, strew the face of the country. Young colts, however fine the stock, had their throats cut. One informant tells us that in one pile he counted forty slain mules on the banks of the Saluda. Every vehicle which could not be carried away was destroyed.

But there were barbarities reported in the more isolated farm settlements and country houses. Horrid narratives of rape are given which we dare not attempt to individualize.

Individuals suspected of having concealed large sums of money, were hung up repeatedly, until almost in the agonies of death and to escape the torture, they confessed where the deposit had been made.

A German baker had a rope put around his neck, and was hauled up several times; until, through fear of death, he confessed that he had specie around his person and in a trunk.

A family of the name Fox, of Lexington, were treated with especial cruelty. The head of the family was hung up thrice by the neck till nearly dead, when he yielded nine thousand dollars in specie.

Mr. Meetze, of the same District, is reported to have been robbed in like manner and by the same process; and one poor idiot —a crazy creature, mistaken for another party, was subjected, till nearly dead, to the same treatment.

This mode of torture, from what we can learn. was frequently resorted to. Other parties were whipped; others buffeted or knocked down, and, indeed, every form of brutality seems to have been put in practice, whenever cupidity was sharpened into rage by denial or disappointment.

But we sicken at the farther recital of these cruelties.

CHAPTER XXVII.
CONCLUSION.

The reader will have seen that we have brought to a close our narrative of the most conspicuous events, in the "capture, sack, and burning of the city of Columbia." We have been at great pains to make the statements ample, and to justify them by reference to the best authorities and witnesses to be found. We believe that the facts are substantially complete, and so, true in all respects. The incidents given are selected as typical of large groups of facts, representative anecdotes, uniform in their variety, and quite too numerous for separate consideration. But the very uniformity, amidst such a numerous collection, is in confirmation of the general authenticity of the whole; and we repeat the conviction that the narrative is wholly true withal, and to be relied on as a history.

We have seen, with surprise, some attempts, in sundry quarters, to account for the destruction of Columbia by ascribing it to accident, to the drunkenness of straggling parties, to our negroes, and, indeed, to any but the proper cause. It is evidently the design of these writers, without inquiring into the motives by which they were governed, to relieve General Sherman and his army from the imputation.[16] If it could be shown that one-half of the army were not actually engaged in firing the houses in twenty places at once, while the other half were not quiet spectators, indifferently looking on, there might be some shrewdness in this suggestion. If it could be shown that the whiskey found its way out of stores and cellars, grappled with the soldiers and poured itself down their throats, then they are relieved of the responsibility. If it can be proved that the negroes were not terrified by the presence of these soldiers, in such large numbers, and did not, (as they almost invariably did) on the night of the fire, skulk away into their cabins, lying quite low, and keeping as dark as possible, we might listen to this suggestion, and perhaps admit its plausibility. But why did the soldiers prevent the firemen from extinguishing the fire as they strove to do? Why did they cut the hose as soon as it was brought into the streets? Why did they not assist in extinguishing the flames? Why, with twenty thousand men encamped in the streets, did they suffer the stragglers to succeed in a work of such extent? Why did they suffer the men to break into the stores and drink the liquor wherever it was found? And

---

[16] The most despicable of all the false charges made was that made in an official report by Sherman that the fire started from cotton which General Hampton had ordered piled in the streets and burned. Hampton's letter to Sherman answering the charge was sufficient to disprove the charge to the satisfaction of any open minded, honest person. But Sherman's frank admission in his *Memoirs*, Volume II, page 287, shows how utterly untruthful he was and how low he would stoop to further injure those he had wronged: "In my official report of this conflagration I distinctly charged it to General Wade Hampton, and confess I did so pointedly to shake the faith of his people in him, for he was in my opinion a braggart and professed to be the special champion of South Carolina."

what shall we say to the universal plundering, which was a part of the object attained through the means of fire? Why, above all, did they, with their guards massed at every corner, suffer the negroes to do this work? These questions answered, it will be seen that all these suggestions are sheer nonsense. To give them plausibility, we have been told, among other mis-statements, that General Sherman himself was burned out of his own selected quarters, no less than four times. This is simply ridiculous. He was burned out in no single instance.[17] None of his generals was burned out. The houses chosen for their abodes, were carefully selected, and the fire was kept from approaching them in any single instance.

But we have pursued our narrative very imperfectly, if our array of facts be not such as conclusively to show that the destruction of the city was a deliberately designed thing, inflexibly fixed from the beginning, and its fate sufficiently well known to be conceived and comprehended by all the army.

Long before the army left Savannah, a lady inquired of one of the Federal Generals in that city, whither she should retire— mentioning her preference of Columbia. His reply was significant. "Go anywhere but to Columbia." We have stated the conference between the Lady Superior of the Ursuline Convent, and a certain Major of the Federals, who originally belonged to the press gang of Detroit. He warned her at 11 o'clock of Friday, "that she would need all the guard he had brought, *as Columbia was a doomed city.*"

A lady in one of our upper districts, expressing surprise at the treatment of Columbia in this nineteenth, or boasted century of civilization, was answered: "South Carolina has been long since the promised boon of Sherman's army."

Masonic brethren told others in the city that an order had been issued to the troops before they crossed the river, giving them license to sack, plunder and destroy for the space of thirty-six hours, and that Columbia was destined to destruction. A sick Federal soldier, who had been fed, nursed and kindly treated by a city lady, told her, on Friday morning, that the place would be destroyed that night. The simultaneous breaking out

---

[17] Sherman's headquarters was the handsome new mansion of Mr. William Talley at 1615 Gervais Street. It is still standing.

of the fires, in the heart of the city, and in the suburbs in twenty places besides, should conclude all doubt.

1.   Enough that Sherman's army was under perfect discipline. They were, as an army, completely in the hands of the officers. Never was discipline more complete—never authority more absolute.

2.   That the fire was permitted, whether set by drunken stragglers or negroes, to go on, and Sherman's soldiers prevented, by their active opposition, efforts of the firemen, while thousands looked on in perfect serenity, seeming totally indifferent to the event.

3.   That soldiers, quite sober, were seen in hundreds of cases busily engaged in setting fire, well provided with all the implements and agencies.

4.   That they treated with violence the citizens who strove to arrest the flames.

5.   They when entreated and exhorted by citizens to arrest the incendiaries and prevent the catastrophe, at the very outset, the officers, in many cases, treated the applicants cavalierly, and gave no heed to their application.

6.   That, during the raging of the flames, the act was justified by a reference to the course of South Carolina in originating the secession movement.

7.   That the general officers themselves held aloof until near the close of the scene and of the night. That General Sherman knew what was going on, yet kept aloof and made no effort to arrest it, until daylight on Saturday, ought of itself, to be conclusive.

8.   That, with his army under such admirable discipline, he could have arrested it at any moment; and that he did arrest it, when it pleased him to do so, even at the raising of a finger, at the tap of a drum, at the blast of a single trumpet.

But, what need of these and a thousand other suggestive reasons, to establish a charge which might be assumed from a survey of Sherman's general progress, from the moment when he entered South Carolina? The march of his army was a continued flame—the tread of his horse was devastation. On what plea was the picturesque village of Barnwell destroyed? We had no army there for its defence; no issue of strength in its neighborhood had excited the passions of the combatants. Yet it was plundered—every house—and nearly all burned to the ground; and this, too, where the town was occupied by women and children only. So, too, the fate of Blackville, Graham, Bamberg, Buford's Bridge, Lexington, &c., all hamlets of most modest character, where no resistance was offered—where no fighting took place—where there was no provocation of liquor even, and where the only exercise of heroism was at the expense of women, infancy and feebleness. Such, too, was the fate of every farm-house—of six in seven, at least.[18] Surely, when such was the fate and treatment in all cases, there need be no effort now to show that an exception was to be made in favor of the State capital, where the offences charged upon South Carolina had been necessarily of the rankest character; and, when they had passed Columbia—greatly bemoaning the cruel fate which, under stragglers and whiskey-drinkers and negroes, had brought her to ruin—what were the offences of the villages of Allston, Pomaria, Winnsboro, Blackstock, Society Hill, and the towns of Camden and Cheraw? Thus weeping over the cruelty which so unhappily destroyed Columbia, was it that she should enjoy fellowship in woe and ashes, that they gave all these towns and villages to the flames, and laid waste all the plantations and farms between? But enough. If the conscience of any man be sufficiently flexible on this subject to coerce his understanding even into a momentary doubt, all argument will be wasted on him.

Our task has ended. Our narrative is drawn by an eye-witness of much of this terrible drama, and of many of the scenes which it includes, but the chief part has been drawn from the living mouths of a cloud of witnesses, male and female, the best people in Columbia.

The following is a list of the owners and occupants of the houses destroyed:

---

[18] The writer possesses a decanter, given him by his mother, that was one of a pair that stood upon a shelf, with bottles and other objects, in the smokehouse of her parents, in Orangeburgh District. Below that shelf was a trough of lard for family use. Sherman's men removed the cover to the trough and with their bayonets swept the glass objects off the shelf so they would crash together in the lard and render it unsafe for

A List of the Property Destroyed

RICHARDSON (OR MAIN) STREET

COTTON TOWN—WEST SIDE.

William Price. Warehouse filled with cotton.
W. McAlister and R. Keenan, Jr. Dwelling.
James Cathcart. Store and warehouse filled with cotton.
R. O'Neale. Two warehouses filled with cotton.
P. P. Chambers. Warehouse filled with cotton.
Mrs. J. J. Kinsler. Dwelling.
Mrs. Law. Store and warehouse containing provisions belonging to Dr. A. W. Kennedy.

EAST SIDE.

James Crawford. Dwelling.
R. O'Neale. Store and warehouse containing a quantity of cotton.
J. R. Kennedy. Dwelling.
L. D. Childs. Dwelling and out-houses.
The houses of A. Civil and James Tarrar saved.

UPPER TO LUMBER—WEST SIDE

Mrs. Kirk. Store, dwelling, &c., occupied by Mrs. Cartwright.
Estate James A. Kennedy. Storehouse containing Government provisions.
Estate James A. Kennedy. Dwelling occupied by A. Boney, M. P. Brennan and others.
P. H. Flanigan. Store and dwelling occupied by J. Milroy.
G. B. Nunamaker. Store, dwelling, cotton house, &c.
A. Crawford. Cotton warehouse.

---

use. Several pieces of glass were chipped off around the mouth of this particular decanter which was salvaged. All throughout the day the soldiers were trying, by various "Yankee tricks" to get the family out of the house so they could fire it, but they remained together—usually in one room—and saved the house. One trick was to go under the house and call out that they were going to blow it up. One soldier found that he had tricked himself. My grandfather killed many hogs each winter and saved their hair to mulch Irish potatoes with in the spring by burying it. The soldier found the fresh turned earth and fancied he had found the place where treasure was buried and procured a hoe and dug up the hog's hair to his chagrin.

A. Crawford. Dwelling occupied by Mrs. J. Jacobs and C. Agnew.

EAST SIDE.

Kraft, Goldsmith & Kraft. Sword Factory.

Henry Hunt. Dwelling.

Mrs. P. Patterson. Dwelling occupied by Dr. I. D. Durham.

St. Mary's College. Government stores, &c.

R. Lewis. Store and dwelling occupied by R. Caldwell and Government goods.

William Lyles. Store and dwelling.

LUMBER TO RICHLAND—WEST SIDE.

William Hennies. Store and warehouse used as cooper's shop and Government storehouse.

William Hennies. Dwelling occupied by owner, store filled with Government goods.

H. Hess. Store and dwelling.

H. Hess. Store filled with furniture.

Grieshaber & Wolfe. Two stores and dwelling.

Dr. T. J. Roach. Dwelling occupied by Molleuhauer.

M. McElrone. Dwelling.

EAST SIDE.

John Judge & Co. Stocking Factory.

A. Riley. Store and dwelling.

A. Riley. Dwelling occupied by ———.

W. McGunnis. Store and dwelling.

A. Riley. Store and dwelling occupied by P. Pinkerson.

The dwelling owned by A. Riley and occupied by Mr. Huchet was not burnt. [19]

RICHLAND TO LAUREL—WEST SIDE.

Estate John Beard. Dwelling occupied by S. Mathews—store used by State Commissary.

Mrs. J. Blankenstein. Store and dwelling occupied by John Mason.

Mrs. J. Blankenstein. Store and dwelling occupied by M. Thomer and others.

---

[19] This was the French consul's house. It is most remarkable that the fire showed perfect respect for the French flag floating over the house. The wind that was alleged by Hitchcock to have blown Hampton's burning cotton so far and wide showed the same sort of respect for the French flag and did not blow any cotton or other inflamables against that house.

M. O'Connell. Store and dwelling.

A. J. Barnes. Store and dwelling occupied by M. Thompson.

W. W. Purse. Store and dwelling.

R. Lewis. Store occupied by J. Fraser & Co.

R. Lewis. Vacant store.

R. Lewis. Store used for Government stores.

EAST SIDE.

Bishop Lynch. Dwellings occupied by —— Ponsignon and others.

John McCully. Dwelling—store occupied by F. D. Fanning.

H. C. Franck. Dwelling.

Mrs. Law. Dwelling—store used as Government warehouse.

LAUREL TO BLANDING—WEST SIDE.

Keatinge & Ball. Engraving and Lithographing establishment.

Estate C. Beck. Dwelling occupied by Mathew Davis and others.

Dr. F. Marks. Store occupied by ——, dwellings by F. Marks, J. A. Patton and others.

Estate John J. Kinsler. Dwelling occupied by Joseph Sampson and others—store by A. Jones.

Estate John J. Kinsler. Store occupied by H. Reckling.

David Jacobs. Dwelling.

M. Comerford. Store and dwelling occupied by H. Kaufman.

M. Comerford. Store and dwelling.

EAST SIDE.

Boyne & Sprowl. Stone Yard.

Estate C. Beck. Store occupied by J. C. Kenneth—dwelling by N. Thompson and others.

James Brown. Government stores.

Thomas Boyne. Dwelling.

C. Norman. Store occupied by Mrs. Hertwig.

C. Norman. Store occupied by J. Mendal.

C. Norman. Dwelling occupied by J. Mendal.

E. Stenhouse. Store and dwelling.

E. Hope. Store occupied by H. Hunt—dwelling by W. Phelps.

E. Hope. Store occupied by A. Miles.

E. Hope. Store and dwelling occupied by E. Hunt.

E. & G. D. Hope. Store—sleeping rooms occupied by P. Schwartz, A. Kœpper and others.

BLANDING TO TAYLOR OR CAMDEN—WEST SIDE.

R. Bryce. Store occupied by Mutual Supply Association.

R. Bryce. Store occupied by Mrs. DuRoss.

R. Bryce. Dwelling occupied by Mrs. D. C. Speck as a boarding house.

M. Ehrlich. Shoe store and dwelling.

M. Ehrlich. Store occupied by W. Stieglitz.

John Seegers. Store occupied by J. Bahlman.

John Seegers. Store occupied by Miss K. Frank.

Bruns & Eilhardt. Shoe store and dwelling.

John Rawls. Store occupied by John S. Due.

John Rawls. Barber's shop occupied by C. Carroll.

John Rawls. Store occupied by ———.

John Rawls. Store occupied by P. Pape.

W. T. Walter. Store occupied by Mrs. Zernow, dwelling by ———.

W. T. Walter. Express Company, unclaimed freight.

W. T. Walter. Dwelling, unoccupied.

W. T. Walter. Store occupied by L. Blum.

Estate J. J. Kinsler. Store occupied by L. C. Clarke.

Estate J. J. Kinsler. Store occupied by Sill & Sill.

Estate J. J. Kinsler. Rooms in second story used by Evans & Cogswell as lithographic office, third story as Treasury Note Bureau.

EAST SIDE.

Bishop Lynch. Ursuline Convent and Academy.

Bishop Lynch. Store occupied by A. Traeger.

Bishop Lynch. Store occupied by J. Blank.

S. Pearse. Residence.

S. Pearse. Store occupied by F. A. Jacobs.

S. Pearse. Store occupied by P. G. McGregor.

H. N. McGowan. Store occupied by V. Heidt.

H. N. McGowan. Store occupied by Miss Evans.

H. N. McGowan. Dwelling occupied by W. K. Sessford.

Fisher & Heinitsh. Store.

Fisher & Heinitsh. Dwelling occupied by E. Egg.

S. Gardner. Store and residence.

S. Gardner. Store occupied by ———.

S. Pearse. Store—dwelling occupied by J. Barry.

S. Pearse. House occupied by colored families.

H. Henrichson. Store.

S. Gardner.   Store occupied by J. J. Browne and W. Ashton.
S. Gardner.   Dwelling occupied by J. Burnside.
S. Gardner.   Exchange Bank.

BLANDING TO PLAIN[20]—WEST SIDE

Commercial Bank.   Dwelling occupied by H. E. Scott.
Commercial Bank.   Store occupied by Farmers & Exchange Bank.
Thomas Davis.   Store occupied by M. H. Berry and J. J. Cohen, dwelling by—Adams.
Thomas Davis.   Store and dwelling occupied by A. Reckling.
Henry Davis.   Store occupied by Silcox, Bro. & Co., dwelling by George Smith.
Henry Davis.   Store occupied by Hopson & Sutphen, rooms above as War Tax Office.
Henry Davis.   Store occupied by T. & R. Flanigan.
Henry Davis.   Store occupied by J. S. Bird & Co., second floor as Zealy's daguerrean rooms.
Henry Davis.   Store occupied by Madame A. Fillette, residence by Dr. Solomons.
Henry Davis.   Store occupied by R. Swaffield and P. Wineman & Co.
Henry Davis.   Bank of Charleston.
R. C. Anderson.   Store occupied by D. Goldstein.
R. C. Anderson.   Store.
R. C. Anderson.   South-western Railroad Bank.
R. C. Anderson.   Transportation office, second story as Government offices.

EAST SIDE.

Southern Express Company's Office, second and third floors occupied by Madame Rutjes as a boarding house.
Southern Express Company.   Store occupied by John Veal.
Estate C. Beck.   Store occupied by Mrs. D. Jacobs.
Estate C. Beck.   Residence and store occupied by Mrs. M. S. Cooper, Miss M. L. Poindexter, J. W. Gaither and family, and others.
Isaac Cohen.   Store occupied by T. J. Moise and F. C. Jacobs.
Isaac Cohen.   Store and residence occupied by John McKenzie.

---

[20] Blanding was repeated instead of printing Taylor, which is the next street south of Blanding.

G. V. Antwerp. Store occupied by W. M. & J. C. Martin, People's Bank and Reynolds & Reynolds, residence of Dr. Wm. L. Reynolds.

G. V. Antwerp. Store occupied by Dr. P. M. Cohen, G. Diercks, and George Bruns.

Charles Black. Store occupied by W. S. Harral and J. Marsh, residence by J. Chrietzberg.

Dr. M. M. Sams. Store occupied by J. B. Duval & Son, residence of William Watson.

Dr. M. M. Sams. Store occupied by J. F. Eisenman & Co., residence by G. V. Antwerp.

Thomas Davis. Store occupied by John Heise, second and third floors by J. N. Roach and J. Richard.

Thomas Davis. Store by Mrs. S. A. Smith, rooms by I. C. Morgan.

Thomas Davis. Store occupied by R. Henning, residence by Misses Saunders.

Dr. C. Wells. Store occupied by Townsend & North, residence by J. B. Duval and W. Lalloo.

Dr. C. Wells. Union Bank.

PLAIN TO WASHINGTON—WEST SIDE

C. A. Bedel. Store, residence by Dr. D. P. Gregg.

C. A. Bedel. Store occupied by Central Association.

J. C. Walker. Residence and store occupied by Dr. John Ingalls.

J. C. Walker. Store occupied by H. C. & H. E. Nichols, residence by A. Feininger.

J. C. Walker. Store occupied by P. B. Glass.

J. C. Walker. Store occupied by J. C. Walker and Durham & Mason, *Confederate Baptist,* second and third stories by Dr. Danelly, *Southern Guardian,* Masonic Hall, J. B. Irving, J. McGown.

J. C. Walker. Buildings on the alley occupied by *Guardian* Printing Office, F. R. Stokes' Book Bindery, Commissary stores.

W. B. Stanley. Store, rooms occupied by Confederate Treasurer, Quartermaster's Office, Commandant of Conscripts, Treasury Note Bureau, Bingham's Dancing School.

Bank of the State. Bank and Branch.

Independent Fire Company. Engine house.

City of Columbia. Guard House.

City of Columbia. Market and City Hall.

EAST SIDE.

Dr. R. W. Gibbes and J. S. Guignard. Store occupied by Fisher & Agnew & Co.

Gibbes and Guignard. Rooms occupied by Mrs. N. Scott, R. Wearn's daguerrean gallery.

Gibbes and Guignard. Store occupied by A. C. Squier.

Gibbes and Guignard. Store occupied by A. Falk.

Gibbes and Guignard. Store occupied by M. A. Shelton.

Gibbes and Guignard. Store occupied by C. F. Jackson, residence by Elias Polock.

Gibbes and Guignard. Store occupied by P. W. Kraft, and Kraft, Goldsmith & Kraft.

Gibbes and Guignard. Store occupied by W. W. Walker.

Gibbes and Guignard. Store occupied by Commandant of prisoners.

Gibbes and Guignard. Store occupied by J. G. Gibbes.

Commissioner Public Buildings. Court House.

WASHINGTON TO LADY—WEST SIDE.

R. Mayrant. Residence and store occupied by L. Shodair.

R. Mayrant. Store, etc., occupied by C. P. Remsen.

R. Mayrant. Store occupied by Cooper and Gaither.

R. Mayrant. Store occupied by C. D. Eberhardt.

J. Stork. Store, house in rear occupied by Provost Marshal.

Henry Davis. Store, etc., occupied by H. Harmes.

Henry Davis. Store occupied by J. & A. Oliver.

O. Z. Bates. Store occupied by T. Stenhouse, house in rear by D. Kelly and others.

C. Volger. Store occupied by L. Hawley, residence by Madame Volger.

C. Volger. Store occupied by Treasury Department.

J. C. Janney. Store occupied by G. Stadtler.

J. C. Janney. Store occupied by A. Feininger.

Janney & Leaphart. Congaree Hotel, rooms in basement occupied by James R. Heise and Reese's barber shop.

EAST SIDE.

Estate C. Beck. Store occupied by J. C. Dial.

Estate C. Beck. P. L. Valory, lithographic office.

Estate C. Beck. Commissary stores.

Estate J. S. Boatwright. Store occupied by Dr. C. H. Miot.

Estate J. S. Boatwright. Paymaster's Office.

G. V. Antwerp. Store occupied by J. N. Feaster and J. C. Norris, Naval Agent.

G. V. Antwerp. Residence occupied by S. Kingman.

G. V. Antwerp. Planter's and Mechanic's Bank.

L. Carr. Bank of South Carolina.

L. Carr. Rooms occupied by D. Wadlow and others.

Southern Express Company. Store occupied by Joseph Walker.

Southern Express Company. Store occupied by D. P. McDonald.

Southern Express Company. Rooms occupied by P. Walsh and others.

Dr. M. LaBorde. Store occupied by L. T. Levin.

Dr. M. LaBorde. Medical Purveyor's Office.

G. S. Bower. Store occupied by Bee Company, houses in rear by G. S. Bower.

W. & J. Shiell. Store occupied by H. Huffman.

W. & J. Shiell. Store occupied by W. Shepherd.

W. & J. Shiell. Scott's barber shop.

W. & J. Shiell. Store occupied by H. & S. Beard.

W. & J. Shiell. Residence occupied by J. Shiell.

LADY TO GERVAIS OR BRIDGE—WEST SIDE.

Mrs. E. Bailey. Store occupied by J. G. Forbes.

Mrs. E. Bailey. Residence by————————

Mrs. E. Bailey. Store occupied by J. K. Friday.

Mrs. E. Bailey. Store occupied by Wm. Moore.

James Hayes. Residence and store.

Henry Davis. Store occupied by ————————

Henry Davis. Store occupied by P. W. Kraft.

W. McGuinnis. Store and residence occupied by E. Beraghi and D. McGuinnis.

W. McGuinnis. Residence and store by C. Brill.

W. McGuinnis. Store occupied by Mrs. P. Ferguson, residence by Mrs. C. McKenna.

James McKenna. Store, etc.

Jacob Lyons. Commissary stores.

Jacob Lyons. Store occupied by A. L. Solomons.

Jacobs Lyons. Store occupied by Muller & Senn.

Jacobs Lyons. Residence occupied by R. D. Senn.

EAST SIDE.

T. S. Nickerson. Nickerson's Hotel.

T. S. Nickerson. Barber shop by Wm. Inglis.

T. S. Nickerson.   Residence occupied by ———.
H. C. Franck.   Store occupied by Franck & Wickenberg.
T. S. Nickerson.   Store occupied by John Fanning.
T. S. Nickerson.   Commissary State Troops.
T. S. Nickerson.   State Ordnance Stores.
Estate R. Russell.   Store occupied by N. Winnstock.
Estate R. Russell.   Commissary stores.
Estate B. Reilly.   Residence and store occupied by H. Simons.
Estate B. Reilly.   Store occupied by ————
Estate B. Reilly.   Store occupied by P. Fogarty.
Estate B. Reilly.   Store occupied by P. Cantwell.

GERVAIS TO SENATE

Capitol[21] Grounds.   Architect's Office, etc.
Capitol Grounds.   Sheds containing marble and granite pillars,
cornices, machinery, etc.
Old Capitol.

SENATE TO PENDLETON—WEST SIDE.

Mrs. E. J. Huntt.   Residence, etc.

EAST SIDE.

Keeper Capitol.   Residence occupied by T. Stark.

PENDLETON TO MEDIUM

A. Palmer.   Residence, etc.
Joseph Green (colored).   Residence.

WHEAT TO BLOSSOM.

Mrs. B. Roberts.   Residence.
Mrs. B. Roberts.   Two cottages occupied by ———.[22]

SUMTER.

UPPER TO RICHLAND—WEST SIDE.

W. McAlister.   Blacksmith shop occupied by Kraft, Goldsmith
& Kraft.
Mrs. Beebe.   Residence.
R. Wearn.   Residence occupied by M. Hislop.
R. Wearn.   Residence occupied by — Boag.
M. A. Shelton.   Residence occupied by G. W. Logan.

---

[21] State House is the official designation of the executive home of the State of South Carolina, not Capitol.
[22] The only building left standing on the two miles of Richardson, the main business street, was the French consul's home.

RICHLAND TO LAUREL—WEST SIDE.

P. M. Johnston. Residence occupied by A. T. Cavis.

J. Oliver. Residence occupied by John Janes.

Mrs. E. Law. Residence occupied by H. Reckling.

EAST SIDE.

P. G. McGregor. Residence.

P. L. Valory. Residence.

D. B. Miller. Residence.

J. F. Eisenman. Residence.

LAUREL TO BLANDING—WEST SIDE.

Estate C. Beck. Residence occupied by ————.

B. Bailey. Residence occupied by Rev. B. M. Palmer.

B. Bailey. Government stables.

EAST SIDE.

C. A. Barnes. Residence.

Prebyterian Lecture Room.

A. J. Green. Stables, etc.

BLANDING TO PENDLETON.

Mrs. J. Bryce. Houses occupied by colored families.

Mrs. S. Murphy. Dwelling, etc.

Dr. R. W. Gibbes, Jr. Dwelling.

Old Baptist Church.[23]

Mrs. J. Friedeburg. Residence, etc.

S. Waddel. Residence.

G. S. Bower. Residence, etc.

W. F. DeSaussure. Residence.

A. C. Squier. Residence.

Estate J. S. Boatwright. Residence.

J. H. Stelling. Residence, mill, etc.

J. H. Stelling. Residence occupied by J. Roach and J. Richard.

Mrs. C. Neuffer. Residence, etc.

---

[23] The old Baptist Church stood at the southeast corner of Sumter and Plain. Next to the east was the new Baptist Church where the Secession Convention met and organized, December 17, 1860, and adjourned to meet the next day in Charleston. On the day of the general destruction a squad of soldiers rode up to the front of the old church where they encountered Holland Mitchell, the negro sexton. They asked him: "Where is the Baptist Church?" He pointed to the old church (a wooden structure). The soldiers dismounted and set it on fire. That the other church was the "new Baptist Church" to Holland saved it from destruction.

F. W. Green. Residence occupied by Miss H. Bulkley.
F. W. Green. Residence occupied by ——.
W. B. Broom. Residence occupied by C. C. Trumbo.

UPPER.

State Agricultural Society. Buildings occupied by Medical Purveyor.

LUMBER.

RICHARDSON TO SUMTER.

John McCay. Grist Mill.
W. Riley. Residence occupied by employees of Judge's sock factory.
W. Thackam. Dwelling, etc.

SUMTER TO MARION.

R. Wearn. Residence occupied by T. W. Coogler.
J. Seegers. Residence occupied by A. C. Jacobs.
Estate Miss S. Ward. Residence occupied by Mrs. Simons.

GERVAIS STREET.

GIST TO PULASKI.

C. C. McPhail. Government Armory.
Evans & Cogswell. Printing Establishment.

PULASKI TO LINCOLN.

Greenville Railroad Company. Office, Depots, &c.
South Carolina Railroad. Depots, office, warehouses, &c.
Blakely, Williams & Co. Store and warehouses.
Blakely, Williams & Co. Commissary stores.
Estate T. Frean. Store, &c., occupied by M. Brown.
Estate T. Frean. Store occupied by O'Neale & Crawford.
James Claffey. Residence, &c.

LINCOLN TO GATES.

Estate B. Reilly. Residence occupied by negroes.
Mrs. Bailey. Residence.
R. O'Neale. Residence occupied by negroes.
Mrs. Bailey. Residence occupied by Mrs. Harris.
———— Residence occupied by Mrs. Walker.
Mrs. A. Haight. Mary Jones.
Sarah Calhoun. Residence.
J. Taylor. Residence occupied by Julia McKean.

Mrs. E. Glaze. Residence, &c.

ASSEMBLY TO SUMTER.

D. Hane. Residence occupied by a colored woman.
Estate B. Reilly. Dwelling, &c.
T. S. Nickerson. Dwelling.
Mayor Goodwyn. Dwelling.

SUMTER TO MARION.

F. W. Green. Office occupied by William Patterson.
F. W. Green. Residence, &c.
J. S. Guignard. Residence occupied by Chancellor Carroll and General Lovell.
Lecture Room of Trinity Church.

MARION TO BULL.

Mrs. B. E. Levy. Residence occupied by W. R. Taber and others.

RICHLAND

GADSDEN TO LINCOLN.

State Arsenal and Academy.

RICHARDSON TO SUMTER

Mrs. H. Gill. Residence, &c.

SUMTER TO MARION.

William Fetner. Residence, &c.
John Judge. Residence.
Lutheran Church.
James Beard. Residence, &c.

BULL TO PICKENS.

Thomas H. Wade. Carpenter-shop.

GIST.

Government Powder Works partially destroyed.

ASSEMBLY.

RICHLAND TO LAUREL.

William Elkins. Residence.
H. Hess. Residence occupied by T. B. Clarkson, Jr.
James Kenneth. Residence, &c.
Mrs. S. C. Rhett. Residence occupied by Major R. Rhett.

PLAIN TO WASHINGTON

J. C. Walker. Residence occupied by T. Fillette.

Estate J. D. Kinman. Residence occupied by Major Jamison.

Synagogue.

J. T. Zealy. Residence, &c.

WASHINGTON TO LADY

John Stork. Residence, &c.

J. P. Southern. Residence.

John Stork. Residence occupied by ————.

J. C. Janey. Livery Stables.

LADY TO GERVAIS.

J. H. Baldwin. Houses occupied by colored families.

LAUREL.

BETWEEN RICHARDSON AND SUMTER—NORTH SIDE.

H. F. and H. C. Nichols. Dwelling.

SOUTH SIDE.

Estate C. Beck. Machine Shop, occupied by H. Brooks.

BETWEEN SUMTER AND MARION—NORTH SIDE.

Dr. H. R. Edmonds. Dwelling.

S. S. McCully. Dwelling.

Estate E. B. Hort. Dwelling occupied by ————.

Mrs. Holmes. Dwelling occupied by Martin & Co.

Mrs. Holmes. Dwelling occupied by Mrs. Fenley and others.

SOUTH SIDE.

Mrs. Quigley. Dwelling occupied by T. A. Jackson.

Thomas Davis. Dwelling occupied by Thomas Davis and C. Marshall.

BETWEEN MARION AND BULL—SOUTH SIDE.

Benjamin Evans. Dwelling.

BULL TO PICKENS—SOUTH SIDE.

Jacob Bell. Residence occupied by Joseph Manigault.

Estate C. Beck. Residence occupied by Mrs. C. Beck and R. Anderson.

NORTH SIDE.

N. Ramsay. Dwelling occupied by W. J. Laval.

RICHARDSON TO ASSEMBLY—NORTH SIDE.

G. W. Wright. Blacksmith Shop.

R. Lewis. Rooms occupied by Dr. A. W. Kennedy.

R. Lewis. Rooms occupied by Dr. Kennedy, R. Lewis, and others.

SOUTH SIDE.

Keatinge & Ball. Stables.

GATES TO LINCOLN—NORTH SIDE.

Glaze & Shield's Foundry.

BLANDING

ASSEMBLY TO RICHARDSON—SOUTH SIDE.

R. Bryce. Warehouses.

NORTH SIDE

M. Comerford. Warehouse, etc.

RICHARDSON TO SUMTER.

Palmetto Engine House.

Mrs. Ann Marshall. Dwelling.

Mrs. Ann Marshall. Dwelling occupied by G. M. Johnson.

B. Mordecai. Dwelling occupied by E. G. De Fontaine, Dr. Baker and others.

SUMTER TO MARION—NORTH SIDE

Dr. A. J. Green. Dwelling occupied by Mrs. Dr. Ross.

Mrs. Z. P. Herndon. Dwelling occupied by Mrs. B. Mordecai.

SOUTH SIDE

Mrs. John Bryce. Dwelling.

C. A. Bedell. Dwelling.

E. H. Heinitsh. Dwelling.

MARION TO BULL—NORTH SIDE.

James L. Clark. Residence, etc.

T. B. Clarkson. Residence.

SOUTH SIDE

Christ (Episcopal) Church.

Mrs. K. Brevard. Residence occupied by W. E. Martin.

BULL TO PICKENS—NORTH SIDE.

C. R. Bryce. Dwelling occupied by Mrs. McKay.

C. R. Bryce. Dwelling occupied by Harris Simons.

Estate C. Beck. Dwelling occupied by James P. Adams.

BARNWELL TO WINN—SOUTH SIDE.

Mrs. H. English. Dwelling occupied by S. G. Henry.

NORTH SIDE

The Charlotte Railroad passenger and freight depots, workshops, round house, etc., together with several engines and numerous cars, were destroyed; also, a quantity of printing and other material on the platforms. The dwelling house on the premises of the company, used as a boarding house for the employees, was not burnt.

TAYLOR (OR CAMDEN).

BETWEEN HARDEN AND LAURENS.

E. J. Arthur. Residence, etc.

BETWEEN BULL AND MARION—SOUTH SIDE.

W. Van Wart. Dwelling.
J. L. Beard. Dwelling occupied by H. G. Guerry.
Estate C. Beck. Dwelling occupied by T. W. Mordecai.
B. J. Knight. Dwelling occupied by D. P. McDonald.
C. Coogler and Miss C. Daniels. Dwelling occupied by Miss Daniels, Levin and others.

NORTH SIDE.

Estate of Mrs. Logan. Dwelling occupied by F. A. Mood.
Mrs. Fowle. Dwelling.
Samuel Waddell. Dwelling.
Mrs. O. M. Roberts. Dwelling occupied by S. N. Hart.

BETWEEN MARION AND SUMTER—SOUTH SIDE.

Estate B. Reilly. House occupied by colored family.
Mrs. J. Rawls. Dwelling occupied by H. D. Corbett.
Moses Lilienthal. Dwelling.
Samuel Beard. Dwelling.
Benjamin Rawls. Dwelling occupied by Mrs. Brightman.
Mrs. P. B. Smith. Dwelling occupied by H. Schroeder and R. Duryea.
Estate B. Reilly. Dwelling occupied by H. Orchard.

NORTH SIDE.

William Walter. Dwelling occupied by John Lance.
J. H. Carlisle. Dwelling occupied by Rev. Jacobs.
J. H. Carlisle. School room occupied by F. W. Pape.

W. W. Walker. Dwelling.
A. G. Goodwin. Dwelling.

BETWEEN SUMTER AND RICHARDSON—SOUTH SIDE.

John Rawls. Dwelling.
John Rawls. Dwelling occupied by T. D. Sill.
William H. Dial. Dwelling.

NORTH SIDE.

John Veal. Dwelling.
W. B. Stanley. Dwelling occupied by Joseph Marks.
S. Gardner. Dwelling occupied by L. Simons.
S. Gardner. Office occupied by Dr. Davega.
H. Henrichson. Dwelling.
S. Gardner. Telegraph Office.

BETWEEN RICHARDSON AND ASSEMBLY—NORTH SIDE.

A. R. Phillips. Dwelling occupied by Dr. M. Greenland, Mrs. John Marshall, Mrs. M. Whilden, Mrs. P. J. Shingler.

SOUTH SIDE.

Commercial Bank. Office occupied by A. R. Phillips.
Commercial Bank. Office occupied by Ladies' Industrial Society.
Commercial Bank. Warehouse, stables, &c., used by A. R. Phillips and others.

SENATE.

ASSEMBLY TO SUMTER.

W. R. Huntt. Residence occupied by James H. Wells and W. R. Huntt.
Mrs. E. J. Huntt. Residence occupied by ———.
Trinity Parsonage. Rev. P. J. Shand.

SUMTER TO MARION.

M. L. Brown. Residence occupied by ———.

MARION TO BULL.

J. S. Guignard. Carpenter-shops, &c.

PLAIN.

BULL TO MARION—SOUTH SIDE.

John H. Heise. Dwelling.
John H. Heise. Dwelling occupied by M. H. Nathan.
John H. Heise. Dwelling occupied by C. F. Harrison.
John H. Heise. Dwelling occupied by Mrs. G. M. Coffin.

NORTH SIDE.

James K. Friday. Dwelling.

Dr. J. McF. Gaston. Dwelling occupied by David Marks.

Dr. J. McF. Gaston. Unoccupied office.

L. W. Jennings. Dwelling.

Rev. T. E. Wannamaker. Dwelling.

William Hitchcock. Dwelling occupied by J. E. Dent.

MARION TO SUMTER—NORTH SIDE.

Dr. D. H. Trezevant. Office and residence.

Dr. R. W. Gibbes, Sr. Office filled with furniture.

Dr. R. W. Gibbes, Sr. Dwelling.

SOUTH SIDE.

James G. Gibbes. Residence occupied by Dr. Boozer.

SUMTER TO RICHARDSON—SOUTH SIDE.

H. Muller. Residence.

Dr. J. W. Powell. Office occupied by Dr. Templeton.

Dr. J. W. Powell. Residence occupied by ———.

Gibbes & Guignard. Warehouse occupied by Fisher & Agnew.

NORTH SIDE.

Dr. Samuel Fair. Residence and office.

Dr. Samuel Fair. Residence occupied by Joseph D. Pope.

Dr. Samuel Fair. Residence occupied by Miss M. Percival.

Dr. Samuel Fair. Residence occupied by A. Laughlin.

Dr. Samuel Fair. Residence occupied by Dr. E. Sill.

Dr. Samuel Fair. Residence occupied by James Tupper.

Dr. Samuel Fair. Office occupied by Dr. Watkins.

C. H. Wells. Government office occupied by Major Radcliffe.

RICHARDSON TO ASSEMBLY.

R. C. Anderson. Odd Fellows' Hall.

J. B. Glass. Residence and Post Office.

C. A. Bedell. Store occupied by James Smith.

LADY.

MARION TO SUMTER.

Estate I. D. Mordecai. Residence, &c.

Mrs. J. S. Boatwright. Stables, &c.

RICHARDSON TO SUMTER.

J. H. Stelling. Mill, &c.

John Shiell. Residence occupied by W. F. Farley.

John Shiell. Residence occupied by J. W. and N. Daniels.
John Shiell. Stables, &c.
John Shiell. Harry Nutting's Bakery.

ASSEMBLY TO RICHARDSON.

J. C. Janney. Stables, &c.
J. H. Baldwin. Residence.

LINCOLN.

E. R. Stokes. Dwelling and Kitchen.

HENDERSON.

RICHLAND TO LAUREL.

William H. Toy. Residence.

PENDLETON.

SUMTER TO MARION.

M. Brennan. Residence occupied by Mrs. Ferguson.

WASHINGTON.

PICKENS TO BULL.

S. Muldrow. Residence.
C. P. Pelham. Residence.

BULL TO MARION—NORTH SIDE.

D. P. Kelly. Residence.
Methodist Parsonage. Rev. W. G. Connor.
Methodist Episcopal Church.

SOUTH SIDE.

Mrs. G. M. Thompson. Residence.
Mrs. G. M. Thompson. Residence occupied by negroes.
M. A. Shelton. Residence.

MARION TO SUMTER

Dr. A. N. Talley. Residence occupied by Mrs. A. H. DeLeon.
Dr. A. N. Talley. Office occupied by L. B. Hanks.
R. L. Bryan. Residence.
Dr. J. H. Boatwright. Residence.

SUMTER TO RICHARDSON.

Mrs. Kennerly. Residence.
John Bausket. Residence occupied by J. N. Feaster.
John Bausket. Office occupied by J. Bausket and S. R. Black.
Law Range. Office occupied by Enrolling Officer.

Law Range. Office occupied by J. D. Tradewell.
Law Range. Office occupied by F. W. McMaster.
Law Range. Office occupied by W. F. DeSaussure.
Law Range. Office occupied by E. J. Arthur.
Law Range. Office occupied by Bachman & Waties.
Brennen & Carroll. Carriage Warehouse.
J. G. Gibbes. Government Warehouse.
J. D. Batemen. Residence.
F. G. DeFontaine & Co. *South Carolinian* Office.
Estate C. Beck. Warehouse occupied by John Dial; rooms above used as Government Offices.

RICHARDSON TO ASSEMBLY.

The District Jail.
P. J. Frazee. Residence occupied by Mrs. G. Crane.
P. J. Frazee. Carriage Repository.
P. J. Frazee. Office occupied by F. Lance, Dr. Anderson.
P. J. Frazee. Residence occupied by D. C. Peixotto.
R. Mayrant. Residence occupied by Mrs. H. Gladden.
R. Mayrant. Residence occupied by J. Dobbin.
R. Mayrant. Stables.
G. G. Newton. Paint Shop.
G. G. Newton. Residence occupied by W. Williams.

MARION.

Residence occupied by Clarissa May, (colored).
House occupied by colored people.
C. H. Pritchard, Residence.
Lecture Room Washington Street Church.
Andrew Crawford. Residence, &c.
J. C. Lyons. Residence, &c.

BULL.

George Huggins. Residence.[24]

---

[24] This list shows that 265 dwellings, or buildings used as stores and dwellings (about fifty percent being used for both purposes), 107 stores, 58 buildings used as banks, offices, barbershops and livery and sales stables, 15 warehouses and railroad depots, 19 factories, mills, and machine shops, 7 church buildings, 4 school buildings, 4 printing and engraving plants, 5 public buildings and 2 hotels, making a total of 486 buildings, were destroyed with nearly all of their contents.

THE

BURNING OF COLUMBIA, S. C.

A REVIEW

OF

NORTHERN ASSERTIONS

AND

SOUTHERN FACTS.

BY DR. D. H. TREZEVANT.

COLUMBIA, S. C.:
SOUTH CAROLINIAN POWER PRESS.
1866.

PREFACE.

———•———

Much discussion has been evoked on the question as to who is responsible for the burning of Columbia, and the outrages connected with that event. In South Carolina, the author of the crime is known to be Gen. WILLIAM T. SHERMAN; but among communities outside of the State, who have not been made familiar with the facts, ignorance on the subject naturally enough prevails. At the North especially, where the press has chosen to circulate only the one sided statements of its contributors, the public affect to believe that Columbia was destroyed by the Confederate authorities; and books have been written, in which falsehoods are gravely promulgated to establish this theory. The object of the present review is to put all doubts on the subject at rest forever.

The writer of the following pages is one of the most highly respected citizens of South Carolina, and has been a resident of Columbia for more than fifty years. He was present during the most trying scenes of the conflagration, a personal witness of many of the outrages narrated, and as the reader will discover, is in every way competent to handle his subject with a clearness and force which its importance demands.

The articles were originally published in the *Daily South Carolinian* at the request of many citizens have been embodied in a more permanent shape.

F. G. DeFontaine,
Editor Daily South Carolinian.

THE BURNING OF COLUMBIA.

"Who is to blame for the burning of Columbia is a subject that will long be disputed." So writes Conyngham in his history of Sherman's grand march, but I think he solved the difficulty by his acknowledgments before he threw out his question and doubt. That controversy can be easily settled whenever the specifications on which the charge is made, are brought to issue; after issue, the truth will become known. It is very evident that the belief of the writer was fairly made up ; that on his mind, there was little doubt as to who was the cause of the destruction of the city, and that Sherman was the man. In discussing the question, he, by implication, charges Gov. Magrath and Gen. Hampton with being partly to blame; but as the statement which he makes, is founded on an erroneous impression, with the correction of that error it must fall.

In the preceding part of his book there are several circumstances stated which are necessary to be brought into consideration before we follow him in his accusation; and it will be found by his acknowledgment, and that of others, that the city was in the hands of the Yankee army some time before the fire commenced; that they got quiet possession, it having been turned over to them by the Mayor, and that all matters under the command of Colonel Stone were peaceably and properly arranged. There is no mention of any insubordination, and not a hint of a fire existing in the city. Under these circumstances, Stone held the city for about one hour before the appearance of Sherman; and Mayor Goodwyn and Aldermen Stork and McKenzie, certify that when they passed the cotton with Colonel Stone, it was not on fire, nor did it take fire for sometime after the authority was vested in him. The Mayor also says: "Gen. Sherman sent for me the morning after the city was burnt, and said that he regretted very much that it was burnt ; and that it was my fault, in suffering liquor to remain in the city, when it was evacuated." The evidence of other gentlemen will be brought to bear upon the time when, and the manner how it did take fire, for they saw the whole affair. Let me now return to Conyngham's remarks, and it will be seen that as far as possible he corroborates the statement I have just made: "Our march through the city was so orderly that even the Southerners began to bless their stars that the reign of terror was over, and that a reign of peace and security, like that at Savannah was about being inaugurated. Alas! that the scenes of the night should mar so auspicious a beginning." "I spent the evening in the Capitol, looking over the archives and libraries. Part of Col. Stone's brigade—I think the 13th Ohio, Col. Kennedy's regiment—was on duty there. Towards night, crowds of our escaped prisoners, soldiers and negroes, intoxicated with their new-born liberty, which they looked upon as a license to do as they pleased, were parading the streets in groups." No mention as yet of any fires about the town, or of any cotton having been found flying about, or on fire, but he writes: "As soon as night set in, there ensued a sad scene indeed." (This is the time Sherman reports that the fires were in full blast, and that he had called in the rest of Wood's division.) "The suburbs were first set on fire"—by whom? the prisoners and soldiers and negroes for it was not within 500 yards of the cotton that Sherman saw burning, *some assert*, by the burning cotton which the rebels had piled along the streets. Pillaging gangs soon fired the heart of the town, then entered the houses, in many instances, carrying off articles of value. The flames soon burst out in all parts of the town," &c., &c. "I trust I shall never witness such a scene again— drunken soldiers rushing from house to house, emptying them of their valuables, and then firing them; negroes carrying off piles of booty, and grinning at the good chance and exulting like so many demons; officers and men revelling on the wines and liquors until the burning houses buried them in their drunken orgies." I think this looks very much like a city turned over to the soldiery to do with as they please; corresponds with what they said—that they were authorized first to sack, and then to burn it—that they, both officers and men, had so determined, and that it met with Old Bill's full approbation. "The frequent shots on every side told that some victim had fallen— shrieks and groans and cries of distress resounded from every side. A troop of cavalry—I think the 29th Missouri— were left to patrol the streets; but I did not once see them interfering with the groups that rushed about to fire and pillage the houses." Methinks after penning such a description, that there was no occasion to ask "who was to blame for the burning of Columbia." But let us see what more he has to

report: "True, Gens. Sherman and Howard, and others, were out giving instructions for putting out the fire in one place, while a hundred fires were lighting all around. How much better would it have been had they brought in a division of sober troops and cleared out the town with steel and bullet. Gen. Wood's first division, 15th corps, occupied Columbia; Col. Stone's brigade was the first to enter the city and hoist the flag over the Capitol—enviable notoriety had not the drunken, riotous scenes of the night sullied its honor." Is it not somewhat strange that Sherman should have been solicitous about the fire? He had told Gen. Wheeler that he would burn all the cotton, and that as to the empty houses, he paid little attention to whether they were burnt or not. We now come to the question, "Who is to blame for the burning of Columbia is a subject that will be long disputed. I know the negroes and escaped prisoners were infuriated and easily incited the inebriated soldiers to join them in their work of vandalism. Governor Magrath and Gen. Wade Hampton, are partly accountable for the destruction of their city. General Beauregard, Mayor Goodwyn and others, wanted to send a deputation as far as Orangeburgh to surrender the city, and when evacuating, to destroy all the liquors. In both of these wise views they were over-ruled by the Governor, and Wade Hampton, the latter stating that he would defend the town from house to house."

There are two points in these remarks, that require to be considered. It is very evident that Conyngham believed that the returned prisoners and inebriated soldiers, were the acting agents; and that Governor Magrath, and General Hampton, were only blamable, inasmuch, as they did not surrender the city when the enemy were forty miles distant. To the grievous fault committed by the latter in not so doing, we have only to say, that

General Hampton had no command at that time; could have had no voice in the affair; and certainly, could not have overruled the wishes of Beauregard, who was his superior, and alone in office. Moreover, the proposition never was made. I now have by me a letter from Mayor Goodwyn, in which he states, that no such proposition ever came before him. This is the only ground on which Conyngham attaches blame to Hampton, and I think I have shown that he had nothing to do with it, for the subject never was discussed; and so falls the allegation made by Conyngham. Had the charge against Hampton then existed, which has been subsequently made, he must have known of it. He was one of Sherman's aids—was at Headquarters—a writer for the *Herald*, and would not have omitted such news as that. His object was to gather up whatever would create a sensation.

I will add one or two more extracts from the same author, relative to Columbia, and then take the reader back to some of the scenes on the route of the army to that place, to show the *animus* with which it entered Carolina, and the determination of both officers and men, as to the course they intended to pursue; which determination was signally assisted, and strengthened by Shermans own conduct at McBrides plantation. That whole march was characterized by such acts as we would have supposed a body of fiends let loose from Hell might have taken some pleasure in enacting; and as Nichols says in his work on the march, "you will in vain search history for a parallel."

"There can be no denial of the assertion, that the feeling among the troops was one of extreme bitterness towards the people of the State of South Carolina. It was freely expressed as the column hurried over the bridge at Sister's ferry, eager to commence the punishment of original secessionists. Threatening words were heard from soldiers who prided themselves on conservatism in house-burning while in Georgia, and officers openly confessed their fears that the coming campaign would be a wicked one. Just or unjust as this feeling was towards the country people in South Carolina, it was universal. I first saw its fruits at Rarysburg (Purisburg is meant), where two or three piles of blackened bricks and an acre or so of dying embers marked the site of an old revolutionary town; and this before the column had fairly got its hand in."

"At McBride's plantation, where Gen. Sherman had his headquarters, the out-houses, offices, shanties and surroundings were all set on fire before he left. I think the fire approaching the dwelling hastened his departure. If a house was empty, this was *prima facie* evidence that the owners were rebels, and all was sure to be consigned to the flames. If they remained at home it was taken for granted that every one in South Carolina was a rebel, and the chances were the place was consumed. In Georgia few houses were burned; here few escaped, and the country was converted into one vast bonfire. The pine forests were fired; the resin factories were fired; the public buildings and private dwellings were fired. The middle of the finest day looked black and gloomy, for a dense smoke arose on all sides clouding the very heavens—at night the tall pine trees seemed so many huge pillars of fire. The flames hissed and screeched, as they fed on the fat resin and dry branches, imparting to the forest a most fearful appearance."

"Vandalism of this kind, though not encouraged, was seldom punished. True, where every one is guilty alike, there will be no informers."

"The ruined homesteads of the Palmetto State will long be remembered. The army might safely march the darkest night, the crackling pine woods shooting up their columns of flame, and the burning houses along the way would light it on, while the dark clouds and pillars of smoke would safely cover its rears. I hazard nothing in saying that three-fifths in value of the personal property of the counties we have passed through, were taken by Sherman's army. The graves were even ransacked, etc. The scenes I witnessed in Columbia, were scenes that would have driven Allaric the Goth into frenzied ecstasies had he witnessed them."

"As for the wholesale burnings, pillage, devastation, committed in South Carolina, magnify all I have said of Georgia some fifty fold, and then throw in an occasional murder, 'just to bring an old hardfisted cuss to his senses,' and you have a pretty good idea of the whole thing. Besides compelling the enemy to evacuate Charleston, we *destroyed Columbia, Orangeburg,* and *several other places,* also over fifty miles of railroad, and thousands of bales of cotton." This is a very fair admission, and we might rest here and go no farther. After what he has admitted to have been done on the route, to conclude the acts of the army by saying they had destroyed Columbia was giving up the question. On his mind there could have been no doubt as to who burnt the city, and as little as to who was the cause of its being burned.

The enviable notoriety is certainly due to Sherman, and to him alone. Those who did the deed were mere agents, and acted to please a cherished commander; they all stated that they knew what Old Bill, (their pet name for him) wanted, and they were determined he should be gratified.

Capt. Cornyn has also hazarded an opinion as to the burning, and with but little hesitation fixes that act upon Gen. W. Hampton. He is, however, but the copyist and mere echo of Gen. Sherman, and gives no single reason why, he should thus have placed the odium of such an act upon Gen. Hampton. He has, however, made use of some other charges tending to implicate Gen. Hampton, which alone induces me to take any notice of him here. His de-

scription is that of Sherman's *verbatim,* with a few additions and rhetorical flourishes to render it more plausible. Capt. Cornyn in his letter to Archbishop Hughes thus writes: "Shortly after our columns were put in motion, the enemy beat a hasty retreat for the city, burning the bridges as they crossed the river. Here permit me to say that Gen. Hampten, on the 15th and 16th February, had it in his power to save Columbia, and to save his people from the terrible desolation that swept over their city on the night of the 17th and 18th." Again he says "had Gen. Hampton acted the part of a great captain, etc., etc, he would have proposed on the 15th and 16th to have surrendered his army, and country to Sherman, for the promise of protection. I am satisfied in my own mind, that Gen. Sherman would have accepted it, but Gen. Hampton pursued a different and most fratricidal course. On Thursday the 16th February, General Hampton ordered all cotton to be rolled in the streets, preparatory to burning the same." No such words are to be found in the order, but as I shall examine and reply to that part of the accusation against Hampton when I take up Sherman's charge, of which this is but the echo, I will only now say that the order alluded to by Cornyn was given on the 14th, not on the 16th, two days before Hampton was in command. For the same reason, had he been willing, he could not have proposed a surrender, and I am satisfied in my own mind, that Sherman for that reason would have taken no notice of it.

Captain Cornyn states that when he came into the town: "We found several buildings burning when we entered. The cotton in the streets was burning in many places, &c.;" and again: "There were hundreds of bales of cotton in the streets from which the devouring element was hissing forth. So high was the wind that it frequently carried immense sheets of burning cotton ten and even fifteen squares through the air like a burning comet, leaving in its wake fiery desolation." I have only to say to this grandiloquent description, that it is not true. There was no house on fire when the army came in. There was but one pile of cotton burning at 12 o'clock; it was put out by one, and completely. It never blazed again, nor did a single house catch fire from it. Capt. Cornyn was entirely mistaken. There are some other errors in that letter, but they are not worth the trouble of refuting.

Major Nichols next presents himself, and as a staff officer of Gen. Sherman, we may suppose that *ego etrex meus* to be one. His account is very much the counterpart of Sherman's, but he has many remarks and admissions that are peculiarly apropos to the subject, and calculated to lead one definitely to the object sought after, viz: "who is to blame for the burning of Columbia." Major Nichols remarks under the date of 30th January: "The actual invasion of South Carolina has begun. The well known sight of columns of black smoke meets our gaze again; this time *houses* are *burning*, and South Carolina has commenced to pay an instalment, long overdue, on her debt to justice and humanity. With the help of God, we will have principal and interest before we leave her borders. There is a terrible gladness in the realization of so many hopes and wishes." Again, Nichols exclaims: "But here we are; and wherever our footsteps pass, fire, ashes and desolation follow in the path." In speaking of the occupation of the city, "On every side were evidences of disorder; bales of cotton scattered here and there, articles of merchandise and furniture cast pell mell in every direction by the frightened inhabitants, &c." But no mention of anything on fire. Nichols writes: "I began to-day's record early in the evening, and while writing, I noticed an unusual glare in the sky and heard a sound of running to and fro in the streets. Running out, I found to my surprise and real sorrow," (why so after the expressions used above?) "that the central part of the city, including the main business street, was in flames, while the wind, which had been blowing a hurricane all day, was driving the sparks and cinders in heavy masses over the eastern portion of the city where the finest residences are situated. Those buildings, all wooden, were instantly ignited by the flying sparks. In half an hour the conflagration was raging in every direction, &c." It will be perceived that both Conyngham and Nichols state that the fire commenced in the evening, after dark, at the very time that Sherman states it to have been so great that he had to call in Wood's division. It will be observed also, that Conyngham, in his remarks, states "that Sherman and Howard, instead of looking after a single fire, when hundreds were burning around, had better have called in fresh troops and driven the drunkards out with steel and lead." And again, that he says, "*about day Wood's division was called on*, when nothing was left to pillage or burn." It is important to bear these facts in memory, as it will be seen that when Sherman gives an account of the catastrophe to free himself from blame, he changes the whole order of the affair and makes the fires to have been burning all day, but leaping into life and activity when the night came on, and requiring him to call for additional assistance. Nichols says "Gen. Howard and his officers worked with their own hands until long after midnight, trying to save life and property;" we presume, for the purpose of having it presented to them, as he, Nichols has so naively detailed on page 204—the manner in which silver goblets, &c., had found their way into the camp.

Nichols proceeds and states: "Various causes are assigned to explain the origin of the fire. I am quite sure that it originated in sparks flying from the hundreds of bales of cotton which the rebels had placed along the middle of the main street, and fired as they left the city." This is mere assertion; no proof of the fact has been offered; the number is exaggerated, there being not more than fifty bales, and from their own statements, there is every reason to believe that it was not so. It is positively certain that up to half-past eleven o'clock, there had been no fire in the city; and then it had been under the command of Col. Stone for fully one hour. Again, he says: "There were fires, however, which must have been started independent of the above named cause. The source of these is ascribed to the desire for revenge from some 200 of our prisoners who had escaped from the cars as they were being conveyed from this city to Charlotte, &c." Again, it is said that "the soldiers who first entered the town, intoxicated with success and a liberal supply of bad liquor, &c., set fire to unoccupied houses." There has never been any proof offered as to the cotton having been fired by Hampton's orders, or by his men. It stands alone upon the authority of Gen. Sherman's *ipse dixit*. Col. Stone, who had the best opportunity of judging of the fact, has not been appealed to and has made no such report. His evidence would have ten times the weight of Sherman's assertion, as he was the first to enter, passed through the Main street, went by the cotton and saw it, and left his men at that very spot. From thence he went to the Capitol with Alderman Stork. The men left, occupied themselves as men will do, by lounging about the cotton, laying on it and smoking, and whilst doing so, the cotton was discovered to be on fire about one hour after they had been there.

Nichols proceeds with his narrative and writes. "Houses have unquestionably been burned during our march, but they were the property of notorious rebels who were fortunate in escaping so easily; while I have yet to hear of a single instance of outrage offered to a woman or a child by any soldier of our army." We do not know what Major Nichols may consider an outrage, but for a man to catch a lady by the throat, and thrust his hand into her bosom to feel for her watch, or purse, would in former days have been regarded as such. So would the lifting up of a lady's dress, because she was not quick enough in freeing her purse from her girdle, the threats of death and a pistol at her head having alarmed her and caused her to give. I should hardly suppose that even in such an army as was led by Sherman, it would have been considered very chivalric to place a pistol at a lady's breast, and demand her watch and jewels, whilst a companion put another to the head of her daughter and demanded the same. Nor would I deem that man entitled to admission in civilized society, who would insult the feelings of a lady by taking to a room, which he had forced from her, and opposite to her own sleeping apartment and that of her daughter, a negro woman and remain there with her all night and go off with her in the morning; yet this was done by one Capt. W. T. Duglass, a commissary, whose name was mentioned to the lady by his clerk, Mr. Sutherland, with a request that it should be published for that act, and for the theft he had been guilty of in her house as every man ought to be, who took up his quarters in a house and suffered it to be pillaged as hers had been. But what shall I say of the villain who fired the house of a lone woman, and then in the presence of the lady took hold of her maid and compelled her to be subservient to his brutal wishes? Words are wanting properly to designate such an act, and we can only say it would have disgraced even Butler the beast. Yet those acts were committed in many of the houses; in some instances done by officers as well as men; hence the "screams and shrieks and groans and pistol shots" that were heard by Conyngham and related by him on page 331. Still further and more wanton atrocities were committed, such as no one would repeat, and none but the lowest grade of blackguardism could have perpetrated.

So far as the Carolinian lady was concerned, much respect was shown to her person and her character. She was robbed and abused, to obtain her jewels and her money; but the instances of other injuries, though many, were not proportionate to the opportunities. The Yankee's gallantry, debauchery and brutality, were confined to the negro; he affiliated with them; they were congenial spirits; their habits, their thoughts and their natures assimilated; they were their associates in the camp, in the streets and in the ball-room; and it was among that class, that their brutal indelicacy occurred. Neither party felt shame for what passed between them; but like the beasts of the forest, indulged in their caprices wherever they met. It was not unusual to see a Yankee soldier with his arm around the neck of a negro wench, even in the common thoroughfares, or hugging and kissing a mulatto girl, when he could find one so degraded, that she would not spurn him for his impudence and want of common decency.

I will give one extract more from Nichols and then turn to his commander who was the source from which the foul slander emanated, and see on what authority he makes his charge. "In the record of great wars we read of vast armies marching through an enemy's country, carrying death and destruction in their path; of villages burned, cities pillaged, a tribe or a nation swept out of existence. History, however, will be searched in vain for a parallel to the scathing and destructive effect of the invasion of the Carolinas." "Putting aside the mere military question for a moment, there are considerations which, overleaping the present gen-

eration, affect the future existence of the section of the country through which our army has marched!" "Over a region forty miles in width stretching from Savannah to Port Royal through South Carolina to Goldsboro in North Carolina, agriculture and commerce, even if peace come speedily, cannot be fully revived in our day." "Day by day our legions of armed men surged over the land, destroying its substance. Cattle were gathered into increasing droves; fresh horses and mules were taken to replace the lame and feeble animals; rich granaries and store houses were stripped of corn, fodder, meal and flour; cotton gins, presses, factories and mills were burned to the ground, on every side; the head, centre and rear of our column might be traced by columns of smoke by day and the glare of fires by night." "In all the length and breadth of that broad pathway the burning hand of war pressed heavily, blasting and withering where it fell." And such was the act of a band of brothers, anxious for the return of the South to the Union, to restore the friendly relations between the two sections of country. Such were the means used to bring about fraternal concord, to reunite a mistaken people, to restore them to their pristine condition, and insure a lasting peace. It was a most extraordinary device—one worthy of Sherman from whom it emanated, but it really seems more in unison with the views of the officer who while wishing them all in hell, yet was determined to "smelt them back into the Union." Where was the Constitution they were fighting for; where the individualities of the States that had so long been cherished? where those rights so sacred that the general government could not even purchase a piece of land without asking for and obtaining the sanction of the State? All ignored, all gone, all sunk and smelted into the one grand consolidated national government of Sherman, with more absolute power over the lives and liberty of the people than the autocrat of Russia.

From the subordinates, let me now turn to the great leader, whose word was law, and whose nod was destiny. Let us see what Sherman says as to "who is to blame for the burning of Columbia." In the frequent conversation which Sherman had with the inhabitants of the town, he uniformly attributed its destruction to the whiskey which his men obtained, and their subsequent intoxication. In no instance that I have ever heard, did he attribute it to General Hampton, nor in his letters, did he deny his complicity in the affair, until his report to the General Government; then, for the first time, we learned that General Sherman disclaimed having had anything to do with its destruction; that on the contrary, he ordered it not to be burnt. Such having been the fact, it certainly was very unfortunate for the citizens of Columbia, that the Generals views should have been so much misunderstood, and that all the soldiers and officers who came into the city, were under the impression it was a doomed city, and was to be given up to pillage until night; and then at a signal given, it was to be burnt. Such undoubtedly was the prevailing opinion, and a nervous restlessness was to be observed about them, an anxious looking out for an expected event, which they instantly recognized and hailed when the rockets were thrown up, and immediately proceeded to their task. That General Sherman had given his orders to General Howard, to burn all the public buildings, by which he meant all that had been used in the Confederate service, he himself, acknowledges. That he did so before he entered the town, or became acquainted with their position, is also certain; that they were so situated, their cremation would end in one general conflagration, was patent to every one, and the order given for their destruction

was, as a matter of course, an order for the destruction of the city; that General Sherman gave that order he has himself recorded; but in no place has he shown where the order ever was countermanded, or where regarding the safety of the city he had guaranteed, with such a wind as was blowing, that he sought the means to prevent the catastrophe. From the statement of his officers, it was certain that he could have prevented it. It was certain that he made no effort to do so—and absolutely certain that he allowed the very corps who had exhibited the greatest animosity, and uttered the most violent threats to enter the city, remain in it when drunk, and continue there until its destruction was completed, or as Conyngham writes "until there was nothing more to pilfer or burn." The same men who were detailed to destroy it, entered with the belief that it would be peculiarly agreeable to him, as General Howard says. They stated such to be their intention. Stated that their orders were on the appearance of a certain signal, the rockets, that they were to fire and pillage, and to continue until the bugle's sound countermanded the orders, and called in the incendiaries. Such were the facts stated by hundreds of the soldiers, and officers as early as 12 o'clock in the day, and such were the facts that developed themselves on the approach of the evening. General Sherman in his remarks to the Secretary of War, endeavours to exculpate himself, and to fix the terrible accident on another. It is my object, now, to state the charge of the General, and to show to the world that it was not true; and that from all the incidents previous, and subsequent to his entrance into Columbia, he himself and no other was the cause of the destruction of the city of Columbia.

He writes: "In anticipation of the occupation of the city, I had made written orders to General Howard touching the conduct of the troops. These were to destroy absolutely all arsenals and public property not needed for our own use, as well as railroads, depots and machinery, useful in war to an enemy; but to spare all dwellings, colleges, schools, asylum and harmless property. I was the first to cross the pontoon-bridge, and in company with General Howard rode into the city. The day was clear, but a perfect tempest of wind was raging. The brigade of Colonel Stone was already in the city and was properly posted. Citizens and soldiers were on the streets, and general good order prevailed. General Wade Hampton, who commanded the Confederate rear guard of calvary, had in anticipation of the capture of Columbia, ordered that all cotton, public and private, should be moved into the streets and fired, to prevent our making use of it. Bales were piled everywhere, the rope and bagging cut, and tufts of cotton were blown about in the wind, lodged in the trees and against houses, so as to resemble a snow storm. Some of these piles of cotton were burning, especially, one in the very heart of the city, near the Court House, but the fire was partially subdued by the labors of our soldiers. Before one single public building had been fired by order, the smouldering fires set by Hampton's orders were rekindled by the wind and communicated to the buildings around. About dark, they began to spread and got beyond the control of the brigade on duty within the city. The whole of Woods' division was brought in, but it was found impossible to check the flames, which, by midnight became unmanageable, and raged until about 4 a. m., when the wind subsiding, they were got under control." "I was up nearly all night, and saw Generals Howard, Logan, Wood and others, laboring to save houses, etc., etc." "I disclaim on the part of my army any agency in this fire, but on the contrary, claim that we saved what of Columbia remains unconsumed. And without hesitation, I charge General Wade Hampton with having burned his own city of Columbia, not with a malicious intent, or as the manifestation of a silly "Roman stoicism," but from folly and want of sense, in filling it with lint, cotton and tinder. Our officers and men on duty worked well to extinguish the flames; but others not on duty, including the officers who had long been imprisoned there, rescued by us, may have assisted in spreading the fire, and may have indulged in unconcealed joy to see the ruins of the capital of South Carolina." I have already alluded to the orders given to General Howard in anticipation of the taking of the city, and of the reckless and wanton destruction of property that must arise therefrom, and not being acquainted with the position of the houses which were thus doomed to destruction—one of which, the Central Bureau, the third house fired, was ignited by Yankee soldiers, and put out and was again fired, and was the cause of the destruction of the whole block. It was near a large dry goods store and drug establishment, which were also fired at the same time, by a Yankee soldier furnished with combustibles. This Bureau was one of the buildings ordered by Sherman to be fired, and for this purpose several men were detailed. They waited for the signal, and in ten minutes after it was given, the place was in flames. It was impossible that this building could have been fired by the cotton; it was to the northward and westward of the cotton, with a hurricane blowing from northwest. About the same time, the house of Mr. Jacob Bell was set fire to and burned This house was at least five squares to the northward and eastward, and it also was safe from the cotton, but not from the turpentine carried about by the incendiaries. There is no evidence that the order for burning was recalled, and Gen. Howard acknowledged that the troops were under the impression that Sherman wished the city destroyed. I will refer to this hereafter. Sherman says "the brigade of Col. Stone was already in the city and properly posted—citizens and soldiers were in the street together, and general good order prevailed." Except in their stealing, such was the fact and contined so until after dark when the rockets were discharged, and then the whole scene changed. (See Conyngham's and Nichol's account of the conduct of the troops &c.,at that time.) What was it that changed the orderly soldier obedient to his commander, to the midnight assassin, robber and house-burner? Three rockets discharged—the signal agreed on when as the soldiers said "Hell was to be let loose and the city wrapped in flames." But let me take Sherman up in the order of his report. "Gen. Hampton who commanded etc., ordered that all cotton should be moved in the streets and fired to prevent our making use of it."

In his letter to Rawls, Sherman says that in the printed order which he saw, Hampton ordered "that on the approach of the Yankee army all the cotton should be burned." This order which he says he saw, and worded as above is the proof that he offers of Gen. Hampton having burned the town. He has no other. It is the ground of the whole charge, and the one on which all his allegations are founded. Were I to grant that an order had been given by Hampton, it would become necessary for Gen. Sherman to prove that the one he had named was the identical one; and that it gave the direction, and authority to act, which Sherman states; but I am not disposed to cede so much, and I think it can be made apparent, though in his name, that the order did not emanate from him—that he sought to have it countermanded, succeeded in so doing, and had it stopped. That order is dated

HEADQUARTERS, Feb. 14, 1865.
[Special Order No.——]

All persons having cotton stored in the city of Columbia, are directed to have it placed where it can be burned in case of necessity, without danger of destroying buildings. All cotton stored here will be burned at any cost rather than allow it to fall in the hands of the enemy. By order of

Major Gen. HAMPTON.

R. Lowndes, Capt. and A. A. G.

Feb. 15th.

I think it will be difficult to show in that order, any directions to roll the cotton into the streets, or to fire it upon the approach of the Yankee army. It contains nothing of the kind; it is a precautionary order to be acted on if a necessity should occur. General Sherman was too well acquainted with what was transpiring in the army of his opponent, not to know that Gen. Hampton at the time that order was given was not in command—that order is dated on the 14th. Gen. Hampton was put in command on the night of the 16th; he therefore could have had no authority to issue such a one; he was only assisting Beauregard. How that order was printed in his name I know not, and cannot therefore speak. I presume it could be explained, but for my purposes it is not necessary. It unquestionably is not such an order as Sherman stated that he saw—no rolling into the streets—and by it no one was authorized to fire the cotton. It was one of precaution, to be acted on under a contingency, and of that contingency Gen. Hampton was to be the judge. No authority was given to any one to burn it, nor could it have been burnt but by the order of Hampton, who was to judge of the necessity. That he did not issue that order is to my mind very plain, for if he had done so, he would have had the same power that gave the order, to authorize him to withdraw it; but it seems he felt that he had not, for immediately upon taking his command as Lieut. General, he applied to Beauregard to get the order countermanded, as will be seen by the following correspondence. Gen. Hampton writes to Gen. Beauregard as follows :

April 22, 1866.

"Gen. Sherman having charged me in his official report with the destruction of Columbia, and having reiterated the same falsehood in a recent letter to Benj. Ravls of that city, may I beg you to state such facts in reference to this matter as are in your possession. If you recollect, I advised you on the morning the Yankees came in, not to burn the cotton as this would endanger the town. I stated that as they had destroyed the railroad they could not remove the cotton. Upon this representation you directed me to issue an order that the cotton should not be burned. This I did at once, and there was not a bale on fire when the Yankees came into the town. You saw the cotton as you left the city, and you can state that none was on fire. Very respectfully yours. W. H.

To Gen. Beauregard.

To which Gen. Beauregard returned the following answer endorsed on the letter :

N. O., May 2, 1866.

The above statement of Gen. Hampton relative to the order issued by me at Columbia, S. C., not to burn the cotton in that city is perfectly true and correct. The only thing on fire at the time of the evacuation was the depot building of the S. C. R. R., which caught fire accidentally from the explosion of some ammunition ordered to be sent towards Charlotte, N. C.

G. T. BEAUREGARD.

Evidence such as this ought to be sufficient to exonerate Hampton from all agency in the burning of the cotton. The fact that he asked Beauregard to countermand the order, evidences that he himself had not authority to do so; and if he had no authority to countermand, certainly he could have had none to order. His asking for that power destroys the validity of the whole charge.

But is the order such as Sherman states it? I think not. It gave authority to no one to burn the cotton. That the cotton was not on fire when Generals Beauregard and Hampton left Columbia is now stated; and the Mayor testifies that when he left the city to go and meet Sherman there was no fire of any kind in the city; and he testifies to the fact that when he came back with Colonel Stone the cotton was not then on fire. Aldermen McKenzie and Stork both testify to the same, and Stork says that he saw the Yankee soldiers light their segars and throw the matches in among the cotton. Upon McKenzie's pointing out cotton to Captain Pratt, and that very pile, Captain Pratt remarked, "I wish you had burnt the whole; it would have saved us trouble, as our orders are to burn all the cotton in the town." Had the cotton been on fire Pratt would have noticed and spoken of it. Alderman McKenzie, who was the Captain of one of the Fire Companies, states that it was some time after his return with Stone and Pratt before the cotton was on fire, and when the alarm was given he proceeded to the place, and never left it until the fire was perfectly extinguished, and the cotton so soaked that it could not again blaze out. Alderman Stork says the same, and adds, moreover, that even the conflagration of the night had not been able to burn it, for it was laying there for some days after. Some was then removed and the rest trodden down and incorporated into the ground. There are hundreds of witnesses to the same fact.

The Rev. Mr. Shand was present when the cotton took fire and I will quote what he says in a letter to me on the subject, and then leave that part of it as settled : "There was a row of cotton bales which *had been loosely packed*, and from almost all of which portions of the fabric were protruding. Along this line of bales there were numbers of Yankee soldiers, *and none but they*—the citizens who were present being confined to the pavements on each side of the street, and at a distance of from thirty to forty feet or more from the cotton. The soldiers were passing to and fro, alongside of the bales, apparently in a state of high excitement, and almost frantic with joy; all, or most of them, with lighted segars in their mouths. I was standing nearly midway between the two corners, watching their movements, when on a sudden the bale at the market end took fire, and the wind being quite fresh, the flames increased and spread with fearful rapidity, and in a short time the whole, or at least the greater part, was in a blaze. The fire engines of the city were brought to the spot as expeditiously as possible and the fire was extinguished in the course of an hour. It was evident that it originated from the fire of the cigars, falling upon the loose cotton. Indeed there was no other way of accounting for it; and another thing is to be noted, that neither sparks nor flames were extended to the neighboring buildings and no damage was done except to the cotton." I will continue the narative of this gentleman as it runs on to the events of the night; since he details clearly the circumstances which occurred and to which he was an eye witness. I have thus fairly shown that General Hampton gave no such order to fire the cotton as Sherman states, nor was its burning attributable to any of his men, or the citizens; but, that it originated from the acts of Sherman's own men, and probably from the very ones who had been detailed for the purpose, and felt that they were performing an acceptable service to their General. I will also state here a part of a conversation which took place between General Howard and Mr. Shand on the burning of Columbia, to which I have elsewhere alluded, and will use the very words spoken. General Howard expressed his regret at the occurrence and added the following words : "Though General Sherman did not order the burning of the town, yet somehow or other the men had taken up the idea that if they destroyed the capital of South Carolina, it would be peculiarly gratifying to General Sherman." Mr. Shand continues ; "The fire was wholly put out by one o'clock P. M., and from that hour until between 7 and 8 o'clock P. M., there was no other fire in the city, and the burning of said cotton, therefore, had nothing to do with the subsequent conflagration and destruction of the town. At the hour last mentioned rockets, were seen to ascend and immediately thereafter a fire broke out in a central portion of the city near the market, and the wind being still exceedingly high, it soon assumed alarming proportions. I stood in my front piazza watching it with much anxiety and though inclined at first to regard its origin as accidental, I was soon undeceived. The fire occurred, as I said, in a central part of the city and to the north of my residence, but I had been looking upon it but for a short time when I noticed fresh flames bursting out in the east, west and south, at points *very distant* from each other and not possibly caused by the communication of flames from one to the other. The revelry of soldiers in the streets and their shouts and exultation, as fresh rockets went up, and fresh buildings took fire, scenes which to some extent came under my own observation, added to the awful character of the occasion and gave rise to the painful impression that the city was doomed to desolation and ruin; a fact which was admitted and boasted of by some of the soldiers themselves. By midnight the whole city presented one vast sheet of flames, and in the midst, and during the progress of the appalling calamity, might be heard above all other noises, the demoniac and gladsome shouts of the soldiery." He further speaks of efforts made to burn his house, their success and their brutal treatment of himself and robbery of the church plate, &c.

Let us follow out Sherman's report. "Bales were piled everywhere, the rope and bagging cut," (no proof of any such being the case,) "and tufts of cotton were blown about in the wind, lodged in the trees, and against houses, so as to resemble a snow storm." This is very poetical, and might give him credit for descriptive powers, but it is too fanciful, and moreover, was not true; after all, it is but a sketch of the imagination. That cotton, which in his eye was flying about in flakes, and adorning the houses with their tufts, was so soaked and soddened, that it did not even burn from the heat of the conflagration of the night, and remained for days on the ground, until it was incorporated with it "by being constantly trodden under" foot. He says "the fire was partially put out by our soldiers;" so far as their labor was concerned, that might be. General Sherman entirely ignores the action of our own firemen with their engines, who did the work, and did it thoroughly. It never blazed forth again, though he writes, that "Before one single public building had been fired by order, the smouldering fires set by Hampton's orders, were rekindled by the wind, and communicated to the buildings around."

I have already shown that Hampton gave no orders, and McKenzie and Stork, certify that the fires did not again kindle, nor was a house ignited by the cotton—but that the houses contiguous to it, were fired in the rear, by Yankee soldiers, who were seen to do so by most credible witnesses. No building was fired from the cotton, nor was it possible for it to have communicated with the first house in flames that night, or to dozens of others which shared the same fate. The pile of cotton which Sherman saw, and to which he alludes, was in Richardson street, near the market; was extinguished by 1 o'clock, and never again ignited. The first fire took place on Gervais or Bridge street, near Gates street, and

occurred immediately after the firing of the rockets. Those rockets were considered to be the signal for destruction; which was anxiously waited for, and promptly attended to. The houses in Gervais street, were the first fired in the city. No fire had occurred after 1 o'clock p. m. Hampton's, Wallace's, Mrs. Stark's, etc., burnt early in the afternoon; they were in the country, and two miles from the cotton—a fact which I beg the reader to bear in mind. The house on Gervais street was about 500 yards to the Southwest of the cotton, and a hurricane as Cornyn says, was blowing. The wind was from the Northwest. Under such circumstances it was a physical impossibility, for fire to have been communicated. On the contrary, a Yankee was seen to fire it, as well as others adjoining. The next house burnt, was that of Bates' and Oliver's, which was near the cotton. No cotton was on fire then. The house was fired in the rear, in Oliver's shoe shop, and put out by a negro who was in charge of the building. The Yankee soldier ordered him to desist or he would beat him. He then fired the house completely, and was seen to do it by several citizens who testified to the fact. The next building, was the so-called public property—the Central Bureau for distributing clothing to the soldiers who were in want. Phillips' ware-house was fired about the same time. This was a block to the North, and the flames could not have ignited, as they would have had to travel against the wind. Then followed Bell's house, five squares off to the North, and East of the others. These premises were all seen to be fired by Yankee soldiers carrying combustibles; and not one was so observed, until after the signal had been given; not a fire occurred from the cotton, Sherman's assertion to the contrary, notwithstanding. After these, fires were to be seen blazing in every direction in the town, and occurring so rapidly one after the other, as to leave no doubt that it was a simultaneous movement, and done by men regularly instructed as to their duty. I could multiply any number of special incidents to prove that the firing was systematic, and consequently ordered. A building, fire-proof on the outside, was being fired within and put out, when the guard told the owner it was no use to struggle against it, as "his house was doomed and had to go." Another, upon removing the fire brand which was put between his floors, was told "to let it alone;" that "the damned house was to burn—it was on the black list." "About dark the fires began to spread and got beyond the control of the brigade on duty within the city." That is true after the rockets were thrown up—somewhere about eight o'clock at night when the fires spread with great rapidity, but no effort was made by the Yankees to arrest the conflagration. The engines were taken from their captains, and so injured as to be useless. The hose was cut, as testified to by Captains Stanley and McKenzie of the fire companies of the city, and the town lay helpless before them; but not a move was made by the Yankees to check the progress of the flames except where a house was burning contiguous to where their officers were staying. Then it would be arrested. Such was the case with Dr. Leland's residence. It was contiguous to Gen. Sherman's headquarters and I think where Col. Stone was stationed. They saved that house, while that of a widowed lady, Mrs. Levy, was permitted to burn by its side—probably because the destruction of Dr. Leland's house would throw the officers out of comfortable quarters. Sherman says "the whole of Wood's Division was brought in, but it was found impossible to check the flames which by midnight had become unmanageable and raged until about 4 A. M., when the wind subsiding, they were got under control." All correct, except one little item, viz: that Wood's division was not called in until between three and four, and they did not fail, but arrested it immediately. Gen. Sherman has been very forgetful of hours in this statement; Wood's division was not called in until morning, and their being called in arose from a little incident which I will presently mention. Conyngham bears me out in the assertion. He says "this scene continued until near morning, and then the town was cleared out, when there was nothing more to pillage or burn." Sherman says, "I was up nearly all night, and saw Gens. Howard, Logan, Wood and others, laboring to save houses etc." I do not question there were many circumstances calculated to render Sherman's rest disturbed, but why he and Howard and Logan and Wood should have tried to save houses rather mystifies me. Sherman had ordered the place to be burnt—Howard was carrying it out—Logan was in favor of the measure, and after he had left Columbia, declared, if it was to be done again, that he would do it more effectually. He also ordered Preston's house to be destroyed. Wood, it would seem, had the command of the forces about the town; and the Yankee writer's state, could have prevented, or have arrested it at any time had he thought proper. That Sherman should be disturbed was perhaps natural; he was not quite demon, and the act he had just authorized was fiendish, though it seem to give him gratification. His officers spoke freely of his disregard for the condition of the city, and declared without hesitation, that he could have prevented it, and could then (two o'clock), stop it by calling in fresh troops, and driving out the drunken soldiers who were disgracing the army. Between three and four, an incident occurred, which led to his ordering in fresh troops, and arresting the conflagration. Then, and not till then, was Wood's division ordered in. Eight hours after the time he stated to the Secretary of War that he had called them in,—they came in, turned out the rioters, and removed the incendiaries. The incident tended much to show the feelings of Sherman, and the course that he had been pursuing. Whilst wandering about the city and admiring the sublimity of the terrible scene, he was recognized by a lady and accosted. She pointed out to him the devastation going on and endeavored to enlist his feelings, by showing the desolation that must follow, and the misery that must overtake so many homeless, destitute families. He told her he had nothing to do with it; that he had not ordered it; that it was her own people who had left whiskey in their way, and given it to the soldiers. She replied,if you have not ordered it, common humanity should impel you to arrest it. He replied, he could not, the wind was so high. She then said, you can stop your men from continuing to fire it; he denied that his men had anything to do with it; said it was our own fault. Whilst making this denial, a servant came up, and informed her mistress, that a man was then setting fire to the kitchen. Sherman asked where, she pointed to him, and he ordered him shot. The guard fired, but the incendiary did not fall, and he caught him and brought him to Sherman who asked if he had not ordered him to shoot him. The man replied, you did, but I did not think you meant me to kill him. There it stopped. The man was ordered to the guard house. He was only performing the duty assigned him; but in the wrong place and time. His fellow soldier knew that he was authorized to do what he was then doing, and so told his commander that he did not think he wanted him killed. After this incident, Sherman gave orders to Capt. Andrews to have the fire arrested, and I beg the reader to remark that the words that were used. I have heard the circumstance told by several who knew of it, and from those who were present, and all used the same terms of expression. Addressing Capt. Andrews, Sherman said: "This thing has gone far enough. See that a stop is put to it; take Wood's Division, and I hold you and them responsible, if it is not arrested." Let us analyze this order. "This thing has gone far enough." Does not that imply, that he was aware of what was going on, and that it met with his sanction. "See that a stop is put to it." Does not that imply that he knew it could be stopped? " I hold you and them responsible if it is not arrested." Certainly this shows that he knew it was under his control, and all the statements made of his inability to stop it, and his regret, &c., proved to have been merely a deception. Sherman says, that, "about dark the fires began to spread, and got beyond the control, &c." At that time there was not a fire in the city, nor did they begin until near eight o'clock after the signal rockets had been thrown up, and then simultaneously in every direction of the city, the houses were to be seen in a blaze. That Sherman ordered the destruction of the city, his soldiers did not hesitate to aver. As soon as they came in, they stated that the city would be burned. That it was settled on the other side of the river between the officers and themselves. That a signal would be given, and then the citizens would "see hell." General Sherman says he disclaims "on the part of my army, any agency in this fire;" but on the contrary, claims, that "we saved what of Columbia remain unconsumed."

After the facts, which I have just stated, I think it will be difficult for any one to give credit to the disclaimer. But as to the saving of what is left of Columbia unconsumed, there is no question that he is entitled to that credit, for after the signal rockets, and until Wood's Division was called in, between three and four in the morning, the city was burning with fearful rapidity; while after the order was given to Andrews, and the bugles sound called the incendiaries from their work of infamy, all became changed. The fire was arrested;

no more houses were ignited; and the destruction of the place ceased. Sherman therefore did put an end to the fire, and certainly saved, by his order, "the remnant of the once rich, and flourishing city." But subsequent events tended to show that he regretted his fit of benevolence. There can be but little doubt that there was an intention to burn the balance when they left; McGregor's house was fired at four o'clock, P.M., on Saturday. Latta's and English's were destroyed on Sunday. Preston's house was ordered for the closing scene on Monday, as soon as General Logan should leave ; and its destruction was only prevented by an accidental circumstance. Major Fitzgibbon, who felt interested in the condition of the nuns, called on and asked if he could assist them. They stated that they had Sherman's promise of protection. He inquired if it was in writing; they replied no, it was only a verbal promise. He urged them to have a written one and offered to carry their request if they would write a letter to Sherman. He was so urgent, and as he stated that the night would be one of horrors, that they wrote to General Sherman, Fitzgibbon, carried the note, and brought them back a written protection, together with guards for their property. His language indicated his belief, that the destruction of the city would be effected that night. Sherman's protection, however, did not assist them. Their establishment was destroyed, and they, and their helpless charge of young girls, spent the night in the church yard. Some ladies seeing their condition, called on Sherman, represented their condition, and urged upon him to render them assistance. He called in the morning, saw the Mother Superior, expressed his deep regret at their loss, and troubled condition, stated that it arose from no act of his, that the conflagration resulted from the liquor which his soldiers had obtained; that they had become intoxicat-

ed and unmanageable; and concluded by offering to give them any house in Columbia they might choose to select for their establishment.

He desired his Adjutant, Col. Charles Ewing to attend to their wants and see that they were made comfortable. That gentleman called often and tried to render their situation more pleasant, and on the eve of his departure, he introduced Captain Cornyn, the Commissary, to them, who was to arrange with them as to their rations. In the course of the conversation, Ewing reminded them of Gen. Sherman's offer to give them any house they would select and urged them accept it; they replied they had thought of it, and would select Gen. Preston's house as being the largest in the town. Ewing replied "that is where Gen. Logan holds his Headquarters; and that house is ordered to be burned. I know that it will be burned to-morrow; but, if you will say that you will take it, I will see the General (he was Sherman's brother in-law,) and get the order countermanded." On the next morning, Captain Cornyn called and told the nuns that the army was moving in haste, and that General Sherman had left the city about four in the morning. They asked if he could tell them whether the order to burn the house had been countermanded, or one given for them to take possession. He could not. After many inquiries, they found, that Gen. Perry had the command of the place, and that his orders were to burn the house at a certain hour, unless they, the nuns were in absolute possession; but he sent them word, if but a part of them came in, he would spare it for their sake. Two of them moved in, and found the fires all prepared, and everything in readiness to burn or blow up the building. The negroes were moving out the bedding, blankets, &c., before it should be destroyed. Here then is rather positive proof that Gen. Sherman paid no respect to his pledge concerning private property. He had pledged himself to the Mayor that person and property should be respected, but here, two days after they had held the city, without any reason that could be assigned, he orders a large and costly house to be burnt, simply because he had the power to show his authority and vent his spleen. Other houses were burnt at the time that was ordered to be destroyed, and we have reason, therefore, to suppose that the man who ordered the one, had also given directions for the other.

It will be seen above that Sherman stated to the nuns that his army was under the influence of liquor, and demoralized. Such was not the fact. The discipline was perfect, and the obedience of the army to the officers exemplary. They never were free from his control; never interferred with each other, and when taken in hand, that discipline was exemplified in their prompt attention to the orders given to Andrews. Their discipline was never relaxed, but certain men were freed from it for special purposes, etc., and it was this freedom that enabled them to commit with impunity all the atrocities of the night; saved them from the patrol, as Conyngham states, and enabled John Hays, of Kilpatrick's cavalry, to go into the country and burn Hampton's establishment. This man stopped at a house to enquire the way, stated his reasons for wanting to know, and remarked that it was his ambition and the dearest wish of his heart to burn Hampton's home. On his return, he called and told the ladies, he had effected his purpose. It was this freedom that enabled them to burn up Wallace's, Stark's and Trenholm's residences. We presume that Millwood, Woodlands and Trenholm's Mills and quarters—places burnt two days after the general conflagration—were also destroyed by special order.

But leaving the city now to repose in its ashes, let us follow Sherman in his career through the country. From Columbia to Blackstocks, there was scarcely a dwelling left. Horses, barns, ricks, shanties, fences, ploughs, all shared the same fate, while the carcases of horses, mules, cows, hogs, sheep, strewed the earth ; killed in the most barbaric wantonness of power. Sherman's advent to Winnsboro, ended in its destruction, but in his report to the Government, he does not allude to its being burnt. Thereby, perhaps, hangs a tale. The why and how might have been demanded, and perhaps he doubted whether Slocum would be civil enough to let him account for it in his own manner. It is certain that whilst Slocum held it, it suffered no detriment. He had pledged himself that it should be protected. It is equally certain that after Sherman arrived there, a considerable part of it was burnt, and not by Slocum's order.

In concluding his account of the burning of Columbia, he reiterates his assertion that it had been done by Hampton, and then goes on to laud his officers and men for their efforts to save the city. He speaks of those on duty, working "well to extinguish the flames," but whilst the army, with its left hand, are making a show of effort, with its right he acknowledges that it was scattering destruction. "Others, not on duty, including the officers who had long been imprisoned, rescued by us, may have assisted in spreading the fire after it had once begun, and may have indulged in unconcealed joy to see the ruin of the Capitol of South Carolina."

Let me now review the assertions of the men and officers as to their orders and intentions when they entered Columbia. We have become acquainted with their object and views on their route to the city. We have seen the woods on fire and the houses in flames, to light them on their way, the cattle killed and the property stolen. The more dark and hidden deeds they have thrown a veil over, but let us see what was the fate destined for Columbia.

The Rev. Wm. Yates states : "I was in the yard when that fatal rocket went up and one of the men exclaimed "now you will see hell." I asked him what it meant, and his reply was: "*That is the signal for a general setting of fire to the city,*" and immediately after, numbers of fires could be seen in every direction." This was at Gen Blair's headquarters and from one of his men. Mr. Shand saw them attempt to fire one of his out houses, and saw them destroy the cotton. Mr. Oliver saw them set fire to Mrs. Law's house, turn Mr. Reckling's wife and child out of his home, and fire it, and also witnessed their firing the cotton. Alderman Stork saw them fire the cotton in the street and also witnessed the destruction of Bates' and Oliver's house. They told Captain Stanley that they would "give them Hell to night;" that they would burn the city, and that the arrangements were all made over the river before they came in. Capt. S., was the captain of one of the fire companies, and whilst working at the fire in the rear of the Commercial Bank, fifteen or twenty armed soldiers forcibly took possession of the hose, stuck their bayonets into them, carried off the pipes, and beat in the air vessel of the engine. He saw soldiers set fire to the Mutual supply association store. Capt. Pratt who came in with the mayor and Col. Stone, told Alderman McKenzie, who showed him some cotton, that he wished he had burnt it and saved them the trouble as they "never left any of that." Mr. McKenzie as captain of one of the fire companies worked at the burning cotton about half past eleven, and continued to do so, until it was completely extinguished. He also assisted in arresting the fire at the jail, which he thinks was fired by one of the inmates. His firm conviction is, that the city was fired by Sherman's men and **through** his directions. Mr. Bedell states that the Yankees set fire to his dwelling house, and that all he could do, could not prevent them from effecting their purpose of burning it. Mrs. McDonald saw the Yankee soldiers break open Mr. Pelham's door and fire his house; Mrs. Squiers saw the teamsters set fire to the cotton opposite De-Sausure's ; she and her family put it out ; that was about half past five in the afternoon. She saw the rockets go up, and immediately after, fires were to be seen in every direction. She confirms what others state, that Bates and Oliver's establishments were fired in the rear, and, therefore, from those houses, spread to the opposite side of the street. Her own house was fired by cotton steeped in turpentine, placed on rods and and put upon the roof. Mrs. Friede bergs house and DeSausure's were all fired about the same time. Mr. Altee says he saw the Yankee soldiers going about and firing the houses on Bridge street and near his own—they twice fired his, but he was fortunate enough to get it extinguished. In one case, it is probable that the enemy would have added murder to their other crimes. A sergeant and three privates went to the residence of F. G. de Fontaine, Esq., the editor of the *Daily South Carolinian*, and demanded of the servants where he was to be found. The latter being unable to give the information, one of the men replied—Damn him, its well for him that he isn't here, for we'd burn him in his den. Then, after ransacking the library, papers, etc., with a lighted candle they ignited the wood work on the place and left it to burn. Subsequently two Federal soldiers were found burned to death among the ruins of the South Carolinian office, in another part of the city. Mr. Pelham, the editor of *Guardian*, was likewise threatened with death in case of capture. I need quote no more. I deem this sufficient to prove that the Yankee soldiers fired the cotton and the houses. Now let us see what they declared to be their intentions. Hundreds of them said to others as was said to Stanley, that they were at liberty to do as they pleased in the town, and intended to burn it to the ground. Two officers, one of the 15th, and the other of the 17th corps, stated, that "they and the soldiers were at liberty to do whatever they pleased; the only restriction was not to injure the women and children." Mrs. Thompson states that her guard told her that before morning there would be no need of a guard for her property as it would be all gone. A captain from Ohio, asked her, why she had stayed in Columbia; said "it was a doomed city; that Sherman had given orders to his troops upon crossing the river, that they were first to sack the city, and then burn it when the signal should be given viz: three rockets." Mr. Thompson states that he was a member of the fire company; that there was no fire in the town when Stone came in; that the fires commenced after the signals, and that the soldiers told him they "always meant to burn it." Lieut. McCroney when conversing with Mr. Harris expressed great admiration of Sherman, and remarked that "he would soon bring the war to a termination; that his policy was to destroy everything by fire and sword in his line of march, and especially Columbia, which he had determined on long before he marched here." A gentleman of Columbia called upon Sherman on the night of the fire to get a guard for the protection of his family and house which was much exposed. He could not see Sherman, but met with Capt. Merrill, who told him that Sherman had given orders to admit no one, and that his seeing him would make no difference, for, "Sherman did not care a damn if the whole city was in ashes." I will now bring this article to a close, after making a few remarks on the burning of the gas works by Gen. Howard under, I may say, the express orders of Gen. Sherman, for such it had every appearance to have been. Mr. Jas. G. Gibbes heard that the gas works were to be burnt. As this was altogether private pro-perty, could have no bearing on the conduct of the war and was not a building useful in war to an enemy; as Gen. Sherman had promised protection to all private property—colleges, schools, harmless houses etc., it was thought that such an establishment ought not to be injured, and that having deprived the citizens of their arms, wood, water provisions and every means of procuring them by the burning of all the mills, and the stealing of all the wagons and horses, they might at least have light spared to them, to enable them to take care of their children who had been so cruelly thrown out of their homes, and deprived of every necessary. This gentleman hearing that Gen Howard had the ordering of its destruction went to him, and remonstrated with him upon the cruelty of such a measure; depicted the distress it would occasion, and the utter wantonness of destroying such a building. Howard replied, that he saw no reason why that should not be burnt as well as the other buildings. He was then requested to postpone its firing until Sherman could be appealed to; he told him he would see Sherman himself; the gentleman asked permission to go with him, as he Gen. H., being in favor of burning, he would not be likely to prove a warm advocate; he declined permission, but said he would see Sherman and try and get the order countermanded. After such a promise we presume he did call on Sherman and endeavor to change his determination. The gas works were however burnt, and we have a right to presume that Sherman gave the order for their destruction, and refused to countermand it. He therefore violated his pledge of protection to the citizen and his property, and committed an act of as wanton destruction as ever was done by man. The burning of those works, the order to burn Preston's house, the destruction of Mrs. English's, Latta's, and hosts of other houses and the utter devastation of the whole country from Columbia to North

Carolina, makes him one of the most ruthless invaders that ever cursed the earth by his presence. Attila or Alaric shrink into insignificance when compared with him; and Nichols was right in saying "that you will in vain search history for a parallel to the scathing and destructive effect of the invasion of the Carolinas." I have elsewhere shown that neither Sherman nor any of his officers had attributed the burning of the city to aught else than the inebriation of the soldiers; and up to the 4th of April, the date of his report to the Secretary of War, no accusation had been made against Hampton. That the charge then brought forward was an after thought, all the antecedents tend to prove. He spoke of the burning as arising from the intoxication of his men—yet on his route through the country, *after* leaving Columbia, he carried out the system he commenced at the bridges below, and kept up during his march to the capital. In his letter to Wheeler, he avows his intention to burn all the cotton, and also his utter disregard as to what became of the dwellings of the planters. To talk of empty houses was ridiculous; from necessity, those houes could have no occupants, though the furniture and slaves evidenced their being cared for, and in fact inhabited. In his letter to Hampton of the 27th of February, relative to the prisoners being shot, &c., he makes no allusion to Columbia; and when Hampton replied, denying all knowledge of any prisoners who were shot after having been taken, he charges Sherman with having burned the city of Columbia after he had peaceable possession of it, and of other matters contrary to the usage of civilized nations. To this charge, Gen. Sherman never replied. At that time he, the great conqueror, never dreamed of being assailed; but, to his astonishment, he found the reverse. At that time he rather looked upon the burning of Columbia as the crowning act of his glory, and for the destruction of our capital he expected something like deification; nor did he awake from his delusion until the rude act of the Secretary of War aroused him from his reverie, and he began to think that he had carried his desire of vengeance too far, and it would be advisable that some cause should be shown to Government why such an atrocity had been perpetrated. It was then he thought of the order he had seen, made his arrangements accordingly, and became satisfied that the city was fully on fire before he gave the order to burn it down through the destruction of the public buildings. Posterity will not be as blind as the present race; their passions will not be excited, and they will acknowledge that Carolina fought, and nobly fought, for a right that she and all the States were entitled to, and had ever claimed; and that, in the infamous desire to crush out her love of liberty and State sovereignty, a tiger had been unchained, who had revelled in blood and destruction, and still continued, and probably would rule until nothing was left of liberty or civil rights to the consolidated but enslaved nation.

I have now done with General Sherman. I trust that I have answered Conyngham's question which I set out to do; that I have removed the slander attempted to be cast on Gen. Hampton by Sherman and his satellites; proved that Tecumseh Sherman was the incendiary, and he, and he alone, is responsible for the terrible destruction that has been occasioned, and the retarding of prosperity for the next fifty years. To his God I now leave the miserable wretch, in the full belief that he will meet with such punishment as his atrocious acts have merited.

Having finished with Gen. Sherman and his *fetes* of arson, let me turn to a few remarks of Major Nichols, in which, contrary to good taste, as well as civility and truth, he attempts to libel the character of the Carolinians. Let me review the statements and the comments he has ventured to indulge in—and I think they will tend fully to portray not only a vile animus, but a miserable baseness of mind. I cannot leave the subject without exhibiting some of his wondrous qualities and gifts.

A portion of what he narrates, he has seen and heard. But when he gives such a description of Hampton, as he has done on page 311, we are compelled to say that he was not acquainted with the man. Of all persons whom I have ever known, and I have known him since infancy, he is the most uniform and imperturbable in his temper. No one ever saw him give way to passion ; his face is one of remarkable quietude and repose, and he is rather reticent than otherwise. In his manner there is a calmness and severity that strikes every one as the predominant characteristic, and a cheerful beaming of the eye that makes the countenance agreeable. You may see determination to do what he considers a duty ; but you need never expect to see restless anxiety or fuss. He is the last being to whom we should have expected such terms to be applied as "fanfaronade," etc. Nichols certainly made a mistake here, and had his friend Kilpatrick in his mind when he drew that picture. He must have recollected the appearance of that officer as Bombastes Furioso, challenging Wheeler out to fight, and imagined that he saw "le petit General," with a flag in his hand, calling over to Wheeler's men, in stentorian voice, "come out now, you set of cowardly skunks; you claim that you whip Kilpatrick every time, come out now and try it; and I'll not leave enough of you to thrash a corporal's guard. I am *Kill himself.*" We almost looked for the boots and the well-known distich and supposed they might have been hung up, if they had not been lost in some of his hurried movements; such as occurred when surprised by Hampton, and in *dishabille*, he ran for the woods, leaving his mulatto doxy to follow

as she could. There are several other remarks of Nichol's that ought to be noticed. Several soldiers were found on the road-side, who had been killed, either by the citizens or by Confederate soldiers. They belonged to a gang who had been firing and pillaging the country in every direction, and simply met he fate they deserved. The virtuous indignation of the Generals is aroused and Sherman gives Kilpatrick orders to hang and shoot prisoners who fall into his hands, to any extent he considers necessary. Nichol's fired on the occasion, calls out: "Shame on Beauregard and Hampton and Butler," and asks, "Has the blood of their father's become so corrupted, that the sons are cowardly assassins. If this murderous game is continued by their friends, they will bitterly rue the day it was begun." Without knowing why or wherefore those men were punished, an order is given for the hanging of the prisoners, though Sherman, when alluding to the circumstance, acknowledges that his foragers committed many acts of atrocity. To the question as to the corruption of the blood of the father's leaving the sons assassins, I have only to say, if Nichol's wishes an answer, he need only ask the question personally, and he can test the condition of consanguinity. Men who have been employed in burning up the country, robbing the houses and turning out the families, to burn their dwellings, are to pass unmolested, because they wear the blue uniform of Sherman's thieves ; but when a rebel soldier fires on one of their officers, although as he states, the poor wretch harmed no one, he was hanged at once for his attempted assassination; a fit commentary upon the statement made above.

A generous enemy would abstain from abusing his opponent, when no longer in the field. An officer of sense may, from want of tact, grandeurize himself and army, but would abstain from depreciating his antagonist. The pusillanimity of the foe necessarily detracts from the prowess of the conquerer, and he who would boast of a victory gained over decrepid old age or staggering infancy; would deem himself heroic in overcoming the coward and the driveller. For his army's sake, for his own share in the *glorious victory won by sixty-eight thousand men over fifteen thousand*, he should not sneer at the conquered, but to enhance his own merit, should make the Carolinians very paladins; the Cids of this century, who fought and defended every inch of their ground with the skill and stubbornness of a Massena. Let me turn to one of the sentences in which he has vented his spleen and exhibited his folly. There are many of the same kind to be found in his work. "A characteristic of South Carolina chivalry has impressed itself upon all of us since we entered the State, and had a marked illustration last night and this morning. I refer to a whining, helpless, craven spirit, which shows itself whenever any of these people get hurt." "These fellows who were to die in the last ditch; who would welcome us with bloody hands to hospitable graves, are more cowardly than children, and whine like whipped school-boys. Ridiculously helpless, they sit and groan, without making an effort to help themselves." That statement is as false as ever was penned by a Yankee, and not a man, woman, or child six years old, but would pronounce the writer of such a paragraph, a miserable dastard, unused to the society of gentlemen, and incapable of appreciating what belongs to the class. The incident that he has mentioned of the Palmetto tree, ought to have made him blush, whilst he was writing such a slander. That tree was respected even by the rude soldier; and why? Because it recorded the names of men who had been engaged in the Mexican war, and brought back with them a character surpassed by none other; because they knew that that Regiment saved the honor of the army, when the troops of New York and Pennsylvania driven back, exhibited their terror to the enemy. They could not advance on Chepultepec, but the Palmetto Regiment, though decimated in the previous fight, advanced against the enemy, supported the retreating forces of New York and Pensylvania, allowed them to regain their *morale*, and enabled Scott to dictate his terms from the halls of Montezuma. Their sons and relatives have met the Yankees time after time in battle, and never given back one inch, with any thing of equal numbers. That they have not degenerated, let Bull Run, Seven Pines, Mechanicsville, Coal Harbor, and a host of other places, testify. Not merely in these places, but you can scarce mention a battle which has been fought, in which the blood of Carolina has not freely flowed. They beat you at Eton, the last battle in Carolina, when Butler drove back your forces. They fought you to the last. * *

Turn to the siege of Charleston—to Secessionville, and say whether any evidence of a craven was spirit there; or whether within the walls of Sumter, the whining of the whipped school-boy has been heard. The siege of that fort should have taught you to have used more truthful language. For more than a year, with your immense force, you tried to get possession of that one fortress and constantly failed. With your immense naval armament and land forces, you day by day, rained your iron balls and shells upon that devoted place, but she succumbed not; you beat down her walls, until she became a mass of ruins, yet still she defied you; and when her upper tiers were silenced and she could no longer return your fire with her cannon, her note of defiance was still heard in the booming sound of the morning and evening gun. Twice you attemped to scale her battered walls, and twice she hurled your forces back, broken and discomfitted; and yet you talk about the craven spirit of South Carolinian chivalry, as an object of the utmost disgust and contempt of the Northern officer and soldier. The expression was as false as it was anxiously desired to be, and in your heart you knew it to be a falsehood. You at last obtained the old fort; but how? Not by gallant conquest, but her own voluntary surrender. She could fight no more and the very flag which you have hoisted in triumph over her battlement, but reads you a lesson of disgrace. The stars and stripes that now flaunt over her battlements, tell you of a flag that had been struck after three days contest, and of others that were arrayed against it for over five hundred days, yet could never for a moment be planted on her soil. And the morning gun but recalls the recollection of that protracted struggle and miserable failure. The assertion was false. No craven spirit was seen in the State; you heard no whining entreaties. They acknowledged themselves overpowered by your numbers, but not subdued by your bravery. They submitted to a necessity forced upon them, and made galling in the extreme by the *grossieries* of of the victors. So far and no farther do they acknowledge. They still believe they were right, but like many others, similarly situated, they have yielded to the necessity of their position. They agreed to remain quiet, but they did not bargain for abuse from the ignorant and the vulgar. The force opposed to them was overwhelming, and their not being able to oppose, reflected neither disgrace nor dishonor. By Major Barry's account, Sherman had 68,000 effective muskets, besides cavalry, etc., and Nichol's himself boasts that the footsteps of 100,000 abolitionists had pressed the sacred soil and broken down our spirits. To such a force was opposed the troops of Hardee, and the few men gathered together in a hurry and concentrated about Columbia—the aged and the boys; in all, not equal to the number that Sherman had in any one of his three Divisions, and 12,000 of these in Charleston, useless to the cause. Under such circumstances, they met and fought you and retarded your movements. To charge a people with cowardice for not beating back such hordes, could only have been made by a brutal mind, regardless of all the amenities of civilization. Let us see, if when he penned those lines, he believed in their truth. Had he forgotten his statement that "the rebels successfully defended their strong line of works on the north side of the Congaree creek, until about four o'clock this afternoon." "Our attempts to cross the river below, have met with earnest opposition." "I never saw more spirited determined fighting, than that of those few hundred brave fellows." If the fighting was spirited and determined on the one side, it must have been equally so on the other, and whilst he has designated the number of those engaged on the one part, why not have said that their opponents were but a few men left to obstruct their march, whilst the rest of the army made good their retreat. Such expressions from any writer, throw doubt upon the narrative; but from an officer it reflects disgrace, and shows a bitterness of mind that delights in traducing. Here let me stop; and I will only say, that I am yet to learn where, with equal numbers and a fair field, the Yankees ever got the better of the Southern Rebels.

APPENDIX.

The following statements refer to the situation of military affairs, and the number of troops engaged on both sides, and have not been embodied in the foregoing account.

The disparity between the forces of the invaders and the defenders of the soil may be thus set forth. If the whole number of men under arms in South Carolina at the time of the entry of Gen. Sherman into the State could have been collected together they would have amounted to about 16,000. Of these, 12,000 thousand were under Hardee, scattered along the coast; 2,600 were under Stephenson, collected chiefly from fragments of the Western army: 1,400 under Wheeler, and 500 under Butler, or say, in round numbers 2,000 cavalry. With this small force it was attempted to hold in check Sherman's army of 75,000 men. Major Barry, the Federal Chief of Ordinance, in his report to Gen. Sherman writes: "The number of guns was reduced to one per thousand effective bayonets. The whole number of field batteries were sixteen, comprising sixty-eight guns, which were distributed as follows: 15th Army Corps, 18 guns; 17th Army Corps, 14 guns; 14th Army Corps, 16 guns; Cavalry, 4 guns. Total 68." Add to to this force the officers, and the probability is that the army must have exceed 75,000 men. Hardee soon withdrew to Charleston, and Sherman started through the swamps, on his grand tour to sever the railroads and reach Columbia. Nichols speaks of the want of spirit in defending the creeks, bridges, etc., which the Federals had to pass, and how they had turned our flank and dashed through woods and water to drive the enemy. He would lead the public

to suppose that desperate assaults had been made against equal forces in which Yankee boldness and stategy had prevailed, when in fact our meagre numbers only enabled us to maintain a corps of observation, which was compelled to retreat whenever the enemy approached too near. In so doing our troops occupied calmly and in order, the next best position to which they were assigned.

If we had had 30,000 men the result, in all probability, would have been far different. Sherman would have been deprived of the pleasure of burning small villages, and indulging in the smaller game of stealing horses, killing cows, hogs, pigs, and sacking hen roosts and negro hovels. From the time Sherman passed Orangeburg there were opposed to him four thousand men, all told—a body which any one of his corps would outnumber by three to one. This small force constantly contested his advance; skirmished with him at Thom's Creek; obstructed his movements at Granby, and held him at bay. As Nichol's acknowledges, "the rebels successfully defended their single line of works on the north side of Congaree Creek until about four o'clock this afternoon," referring to the operations of the 15th, preceding their entry into Columbia. This was done by Wheeler, with about 600 men. Nichols continues: "Our attempts to cross the river below the city have met with earnest opposition. After sharp skirmishing we managed to get a few men across the river in boats. I never saw more spirited or determined fighting than that of these few hundred brave fellows," referring of course to the Federal advance guard. He pays further tribute to the gallantry of our little army in his account of the battle of Averysborough, when he writes, "The regiment of Charleston heavy artillery, made up of the best blood of Carolina, was in our immediate front during the fight. It fought well, and suffered severely, both in officers and men. A larger proportion of officers were wounded in this fight than any fight I have known." Yet these are the men who had lost caste—had become so demoralized that it was impossible to recover their position, etc. He adds further, "The rebels have shown more pluck than we have seen in them since Atlanta. To be sure they were behind breastworks, and fully equaled us in numbers actually engaged; but they supposed the whole army would come up, which was half the battle to us in its moral effect upon them."

With such admissions as this, it is wilful slander and unworthy of any writer, who has the true feelings and principles of a gentleman, to make the statements we have just recorded.

To return, however, to the defence of Columbia. Sherman arrived here with the whole of his immense army, confronted by not more than 5,000 men, all told; a difference of about twelve to one. This small force had been scattered over a space of thirty miles, and was in fact little more than an army of scouts. So if there be any disgrace attaching to the defence of the Capitol of South Carolina, it surely rests on Sherman, who proved himself so dastardly in disposition, fiendish in temper, and brutal in conduct, as to devastate a country wholly incapable of protecting itself and completely in his power. Nor would he have attempted it, had Gen. Johnston been in command with a force of even 20,000 men. For that officer, with about that number of men, afterwards fought Sherman at Bentonville, and for three days held his great army, nearly three larger than our own, completely in check. Unfortunately, South Carolina could not have mustered 20,000 troops under any circumstances. Sherman knew the country was at his mercy and, like a fiend, he showed none. In his recent fourth of July speech, he boasts of having succeeded in effecting the results he intended, and virtually acknowledges

the destruction he has so often denied. In fact, the great idol of the North, spoke scarcely a truth while in South Carolina. What confidence can be placed in a man who thus officially falsifies matters which come under his observation, and disparages an enemy whose prowess he had occasion to fear and to respect on every occasion.

We can only view the march of Sherman through Georgia and the Carolinas, as a Great Raid, conceived and carried out, simply because he anticipated no opposition. Hood's bold and unfortunate attempt in Tennesee left the door open. It was, in fact, safer for the Federal Commander to march to the coast than to retrace his steps. He came to Savannah because there were few or no obstacles in his way; he pressed forward to Columbia, because there were few troops in this direction to contest his advance, and he burnt the city to the ground, to gratify a fiendish spirit which revelled in the misery of his fellowmen. If there is glory in this, let him and his friends make the most of it.

The impartial historian will record that in no single instance did Sherman ever whip Gen. Johnston, or Kilpatrick obtain the advantage of Gen. Hampton. In truth, Gen. Kilpatrick does not figure very boldly in the closing scenes of the war, with all the assistance of Nichols and Sherman. After his famous race to the swamp near Fayetteville, when he took his precipitate departure in his shirt and draws, leaving his fair and frail school marm behind, the great Yankee cavalryman kept well under the wing of the infantry.

I close this brief review of the military operations of Gen. Sherman in South Carolina, with the following extract from a letter written by a distinguished officer, whose position enabled him to obtain correct information, and who moreover was a participant in the scenes to which he refers:

"At Congaree creek not more than 600 men of Wheeler's were engaged, and the enemy only succeeded in dislodging him by crossing the creek above and below them. This fight held Sherman all day, and he camped that night near the Congaree creek. The infantry were withdrawn to the Columbia side of the river soon after dark and were followed by the cavalry. The bridge was burned contrary to orders. The order was for the Engineers to destroy one or two arches. Wheeler's command was placed, one brigade with Butler below Columbia, and the rest on the Saluda river. There were thus in Columbia, only 2600 infantry under Stephenson, Butler's cavalry, about 600 men, and one brigade of Wheeler's, about 400. Wheeler fought at the Saluda, and between that and Broad river, which he crossed on the evening of the 16th. At 3 A. M., on the 17th, Stephenson took Wheeler's place, and the latter marched higher up the river. There were about 4,500 to 5,000 men in all, guarding the river from Frost's plantation to Zeigler's Ferry, a distance of about 30 miles. The enemy crossed during the night of the 16th, in front of the infantry, and Gen. Hampton seeing that all defence was hopeless, ordered Stephenson to fall back. Soon after sun rise on the 17th, Wheeler covered his withdrawal."

An extract from Wheeler's report states that "about nine o'clock or half-past, when near the cross roads, two miles north of Columbia, I met the Mayor of Columbia in a carriage, preceded by a large white flag. I immediately ordered the firing to cease, and allowed him to pass on to the enemy. I withdrew up the Winnsboro road. Gen. Hampton shelled the camp of the enemy from the hills of East Granby on the night of the 15th, and Butler repelled quite a severe attack upon him. The artillery lost six or seven horses killed, and there were quite a number of men wounded.

"From Chester, we turned and got on both flanks of the enemy, and had almost daily skirmishes, some quite heavy. Every day from 50 to 300 prisoners were brought in. The Provost Marshall reported upwards of 3,000 prisoners turned over by the cavalry, and I think nearly as great a number were killed and wounded. About 100 wagons, 400 head of cattle and several hundred head of horses, were captured in the campaign. Sherman's whole loss from the time he left Columbia to the end of the struggle, was not less than 10,000 men. At Fayetteville, about 100 Yankee cavalry came in when none of our troops were there; eight men charged them, routed them, killing eight and capturing nine—the leader and seven men. Near Fayetteville, Kilpatrick was attacked and his camp was taken, with upwards of 500 Yankees and 173 of our men, who were prisoners. Kilpatrick escaped in his shirt and draws only, leaving his fair and frail Yankee school marm, in our hands. One of our boys assisted in dressing her and let her go to her protector. At Bentonville, Gen. Johnston attacked Sherman. Two corps drove him a mile, took three guns, and a line of breastworks. Had his whole force been in position he would have defeated Sherman entirely. With 18,000 men, he held his position in front of Sherman's whole force, strengthened by Schofield's corps for three days, and then retreated without loss. From ——— to Hillsboro, the cavalry were engaged every day, covering the retreat of the infantry. Some of these affairs were quite serious, and all creditable to our army. The day before Raleigh was evacuated, it was desirable to check the advance of the enemy as much as possible, in order to remove the stores, etc. With one brigade only, and Butler's Command, and two batteries of artillery, two corps of the enemy were so steadily engaged, that they advanced only five miles in six hours. When we evacuated Raleigh, Kilpatrick charged Hampton's rear-guard. We turned on him, charged and drove him back in confusion, taking prisoners, and killing and wounding some of his men. This was the last fight of Hampton's command and it was a success."

No r let me ask with such facts before him, Nichols being Sherman's aid, what epithet should be attacked to his *honored name*, when he could pen the following lines.

"The Rebels hope that Johnston will be able to recall and reinforce that army ; but no man living has that power. He might as well try to reclothe the naked limbs of those oaks trees yonder on the hill side, with last years foliage of green ; or a task more impossible yet, restore to the Southern Gentlemen, their lost reputation for chivalry, honor and manhood."